LOVE MAKES EVERYTHING BETTER

ADULT COLORING BOOK

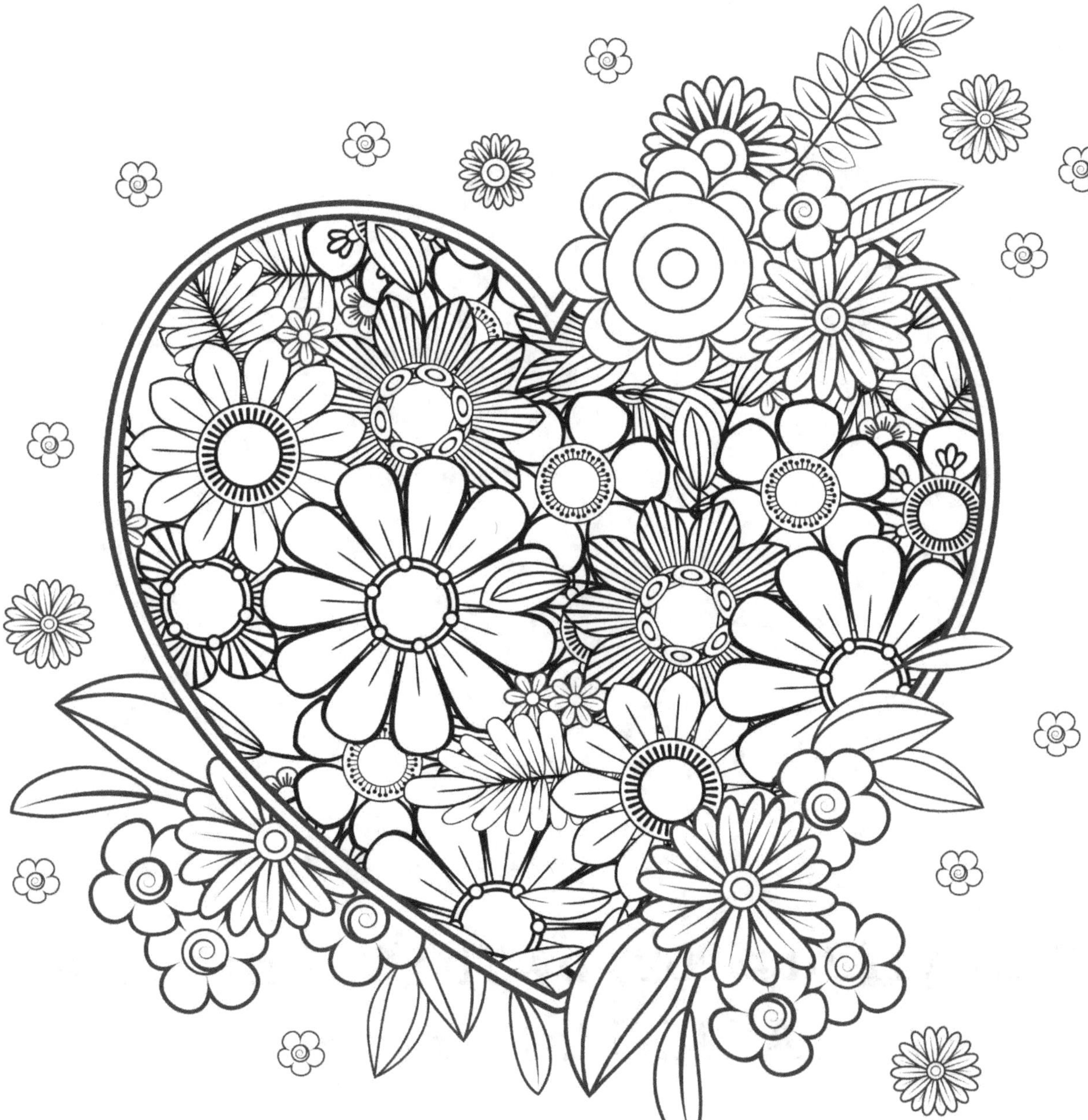

Copyright© 2021 by The Colorful Tree
All Rights Reserved

THIS COLORING BOOK BELONGS TO

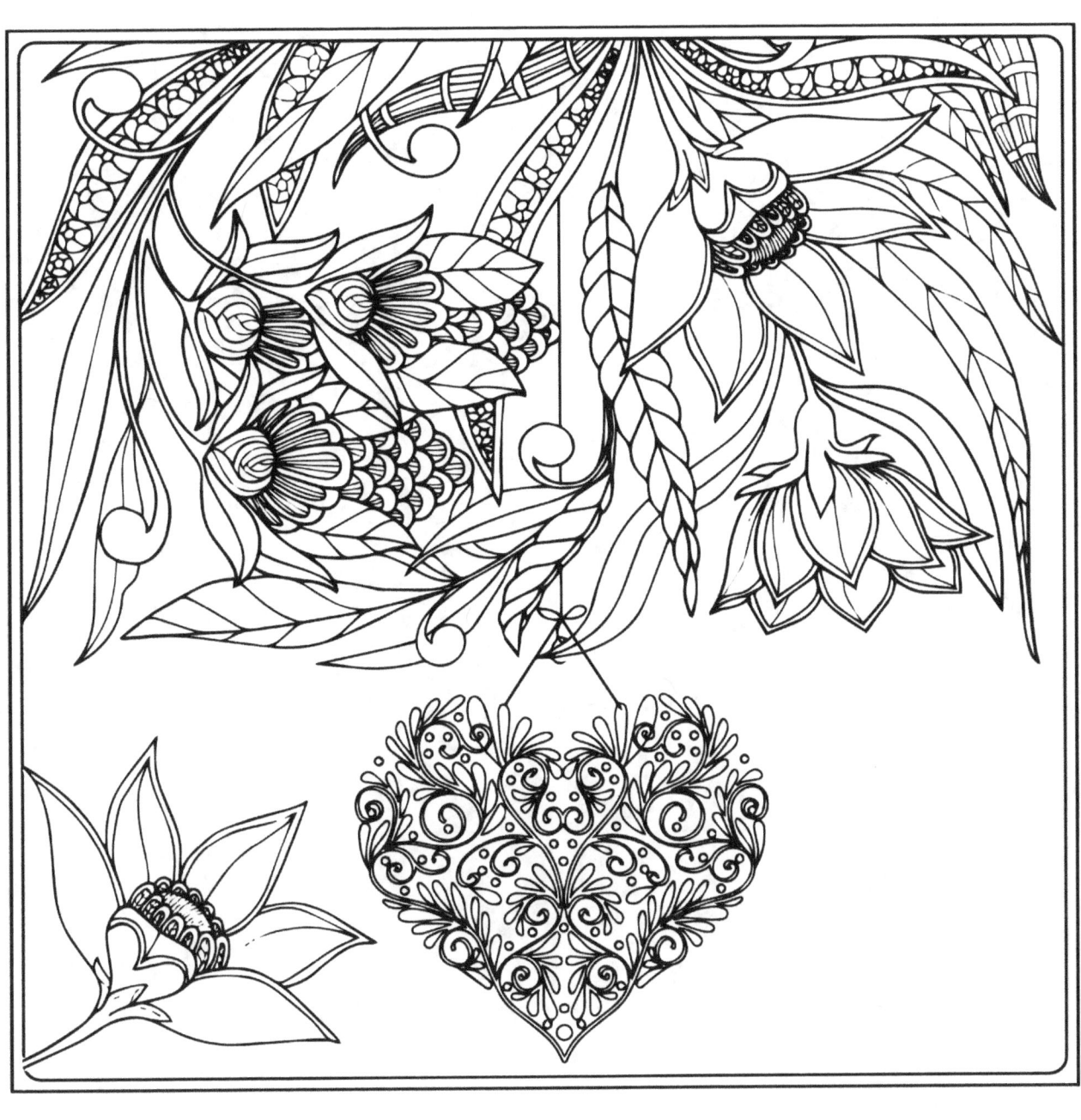

COLOR TEST PAGE

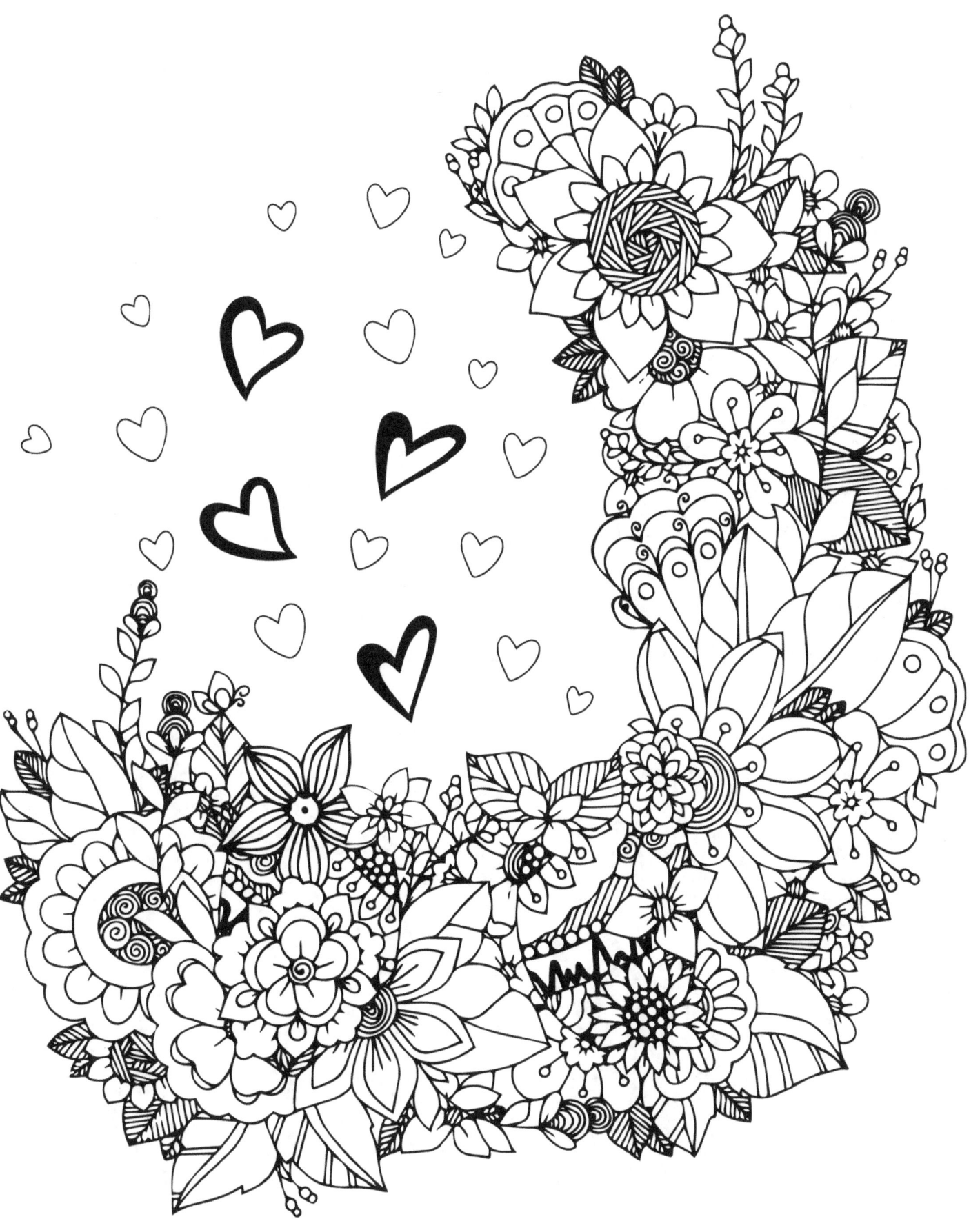

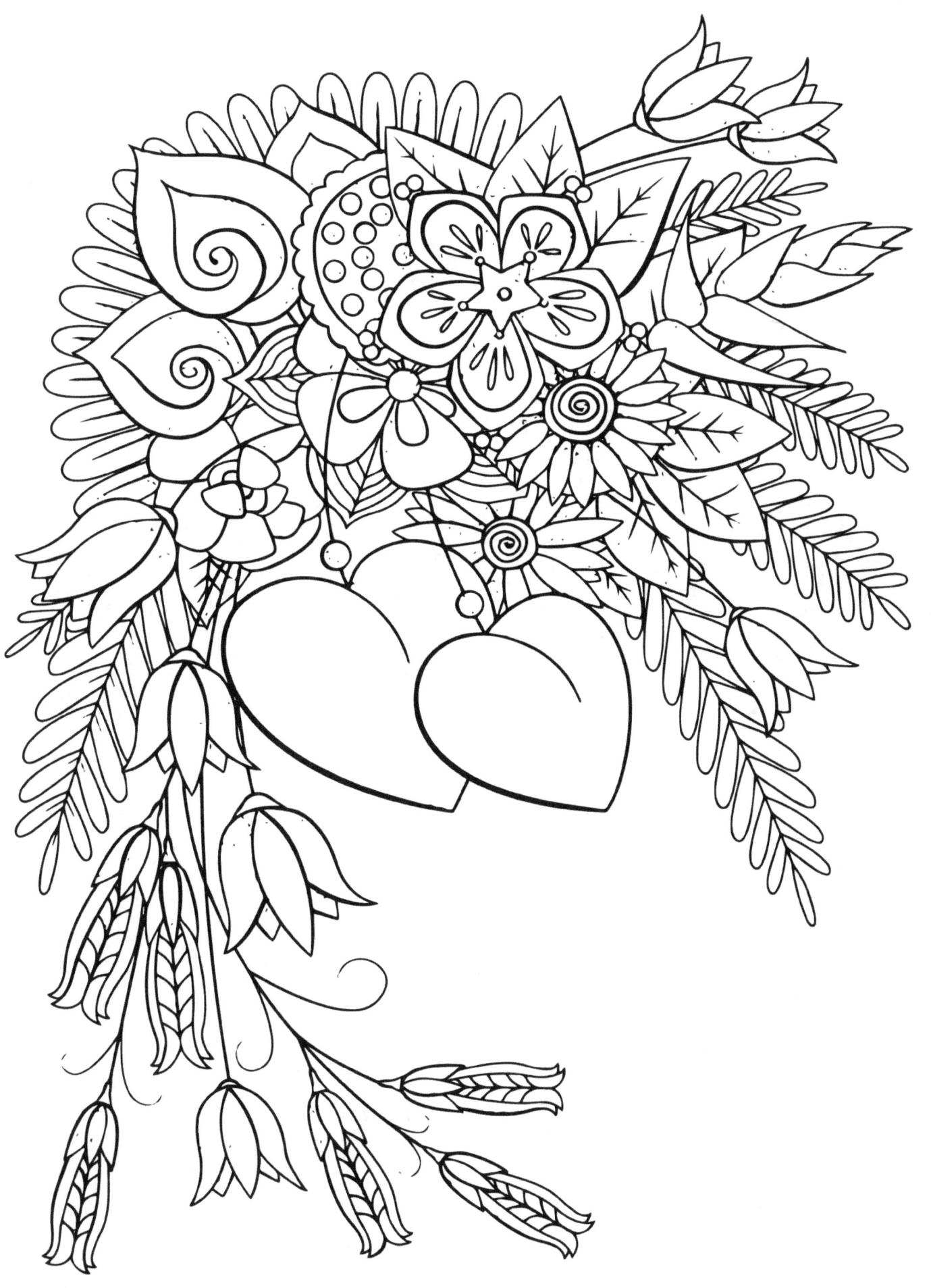

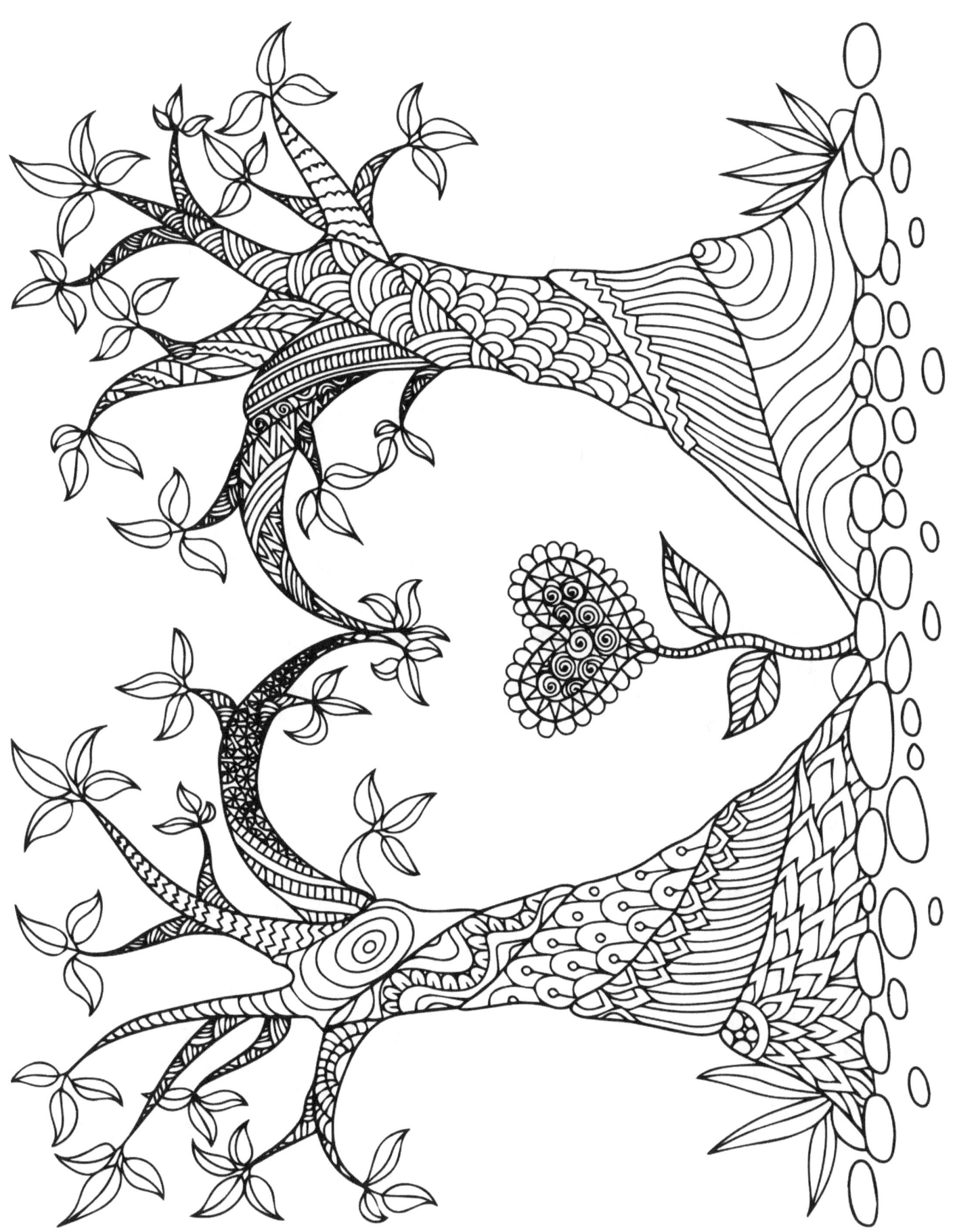

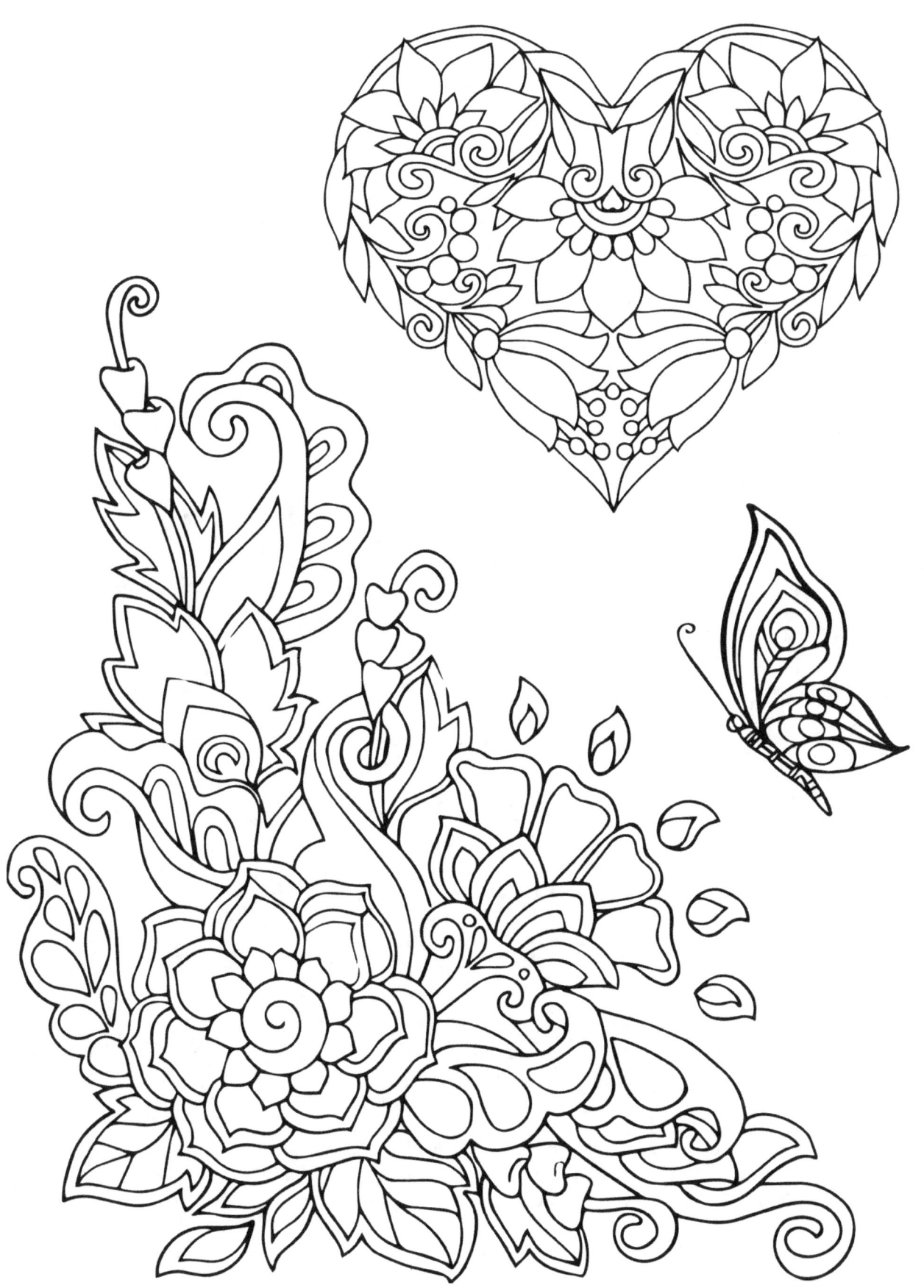

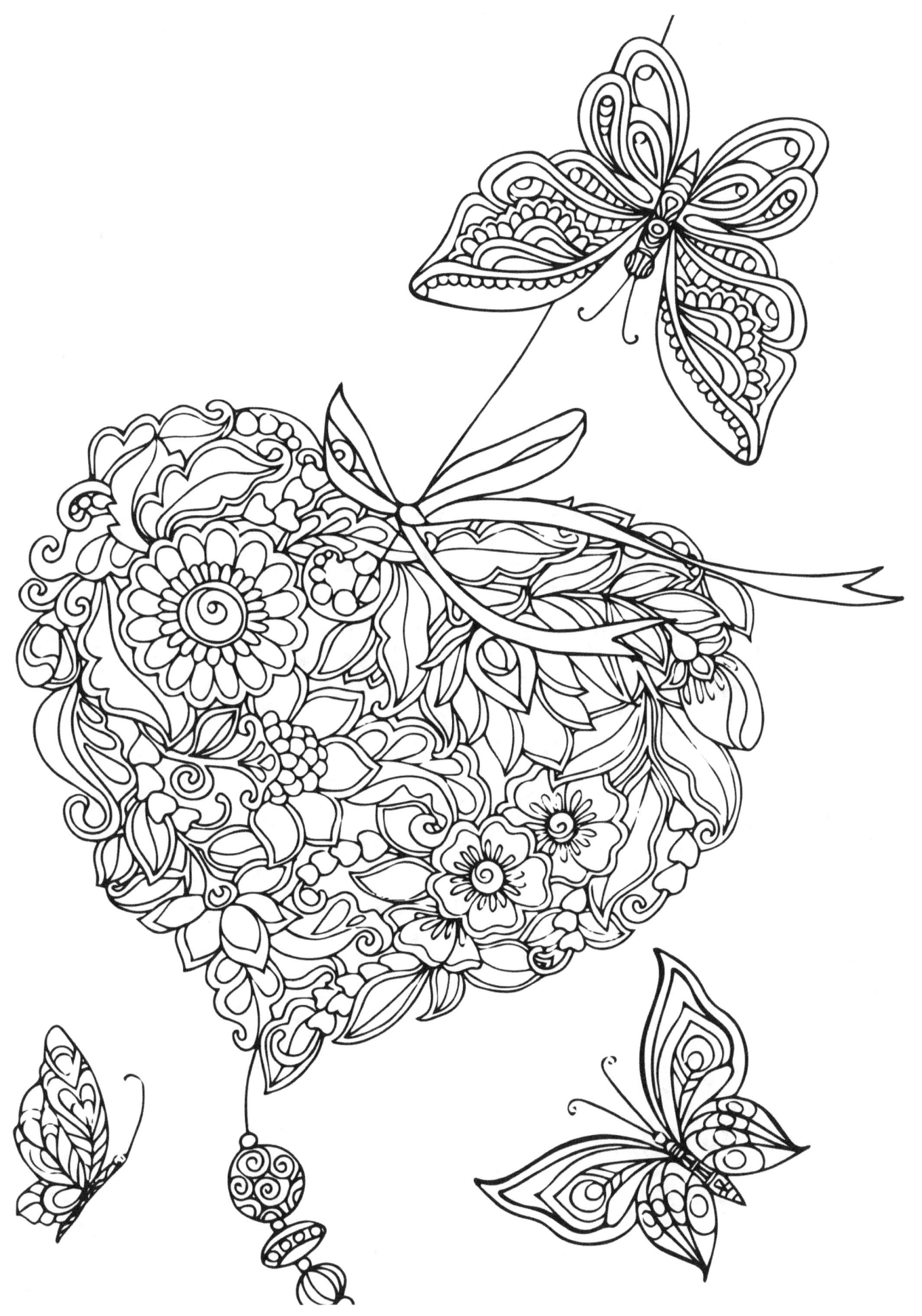

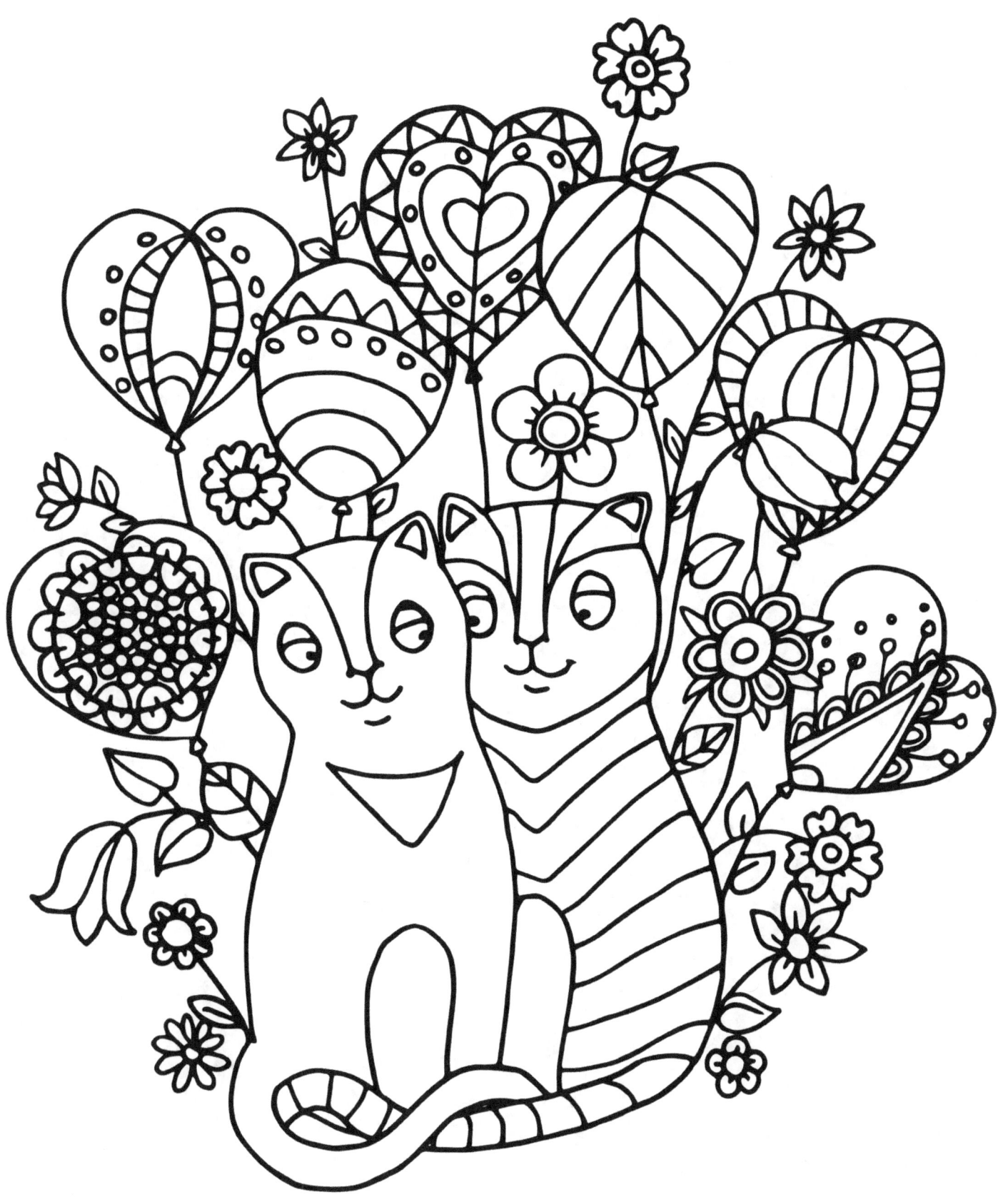

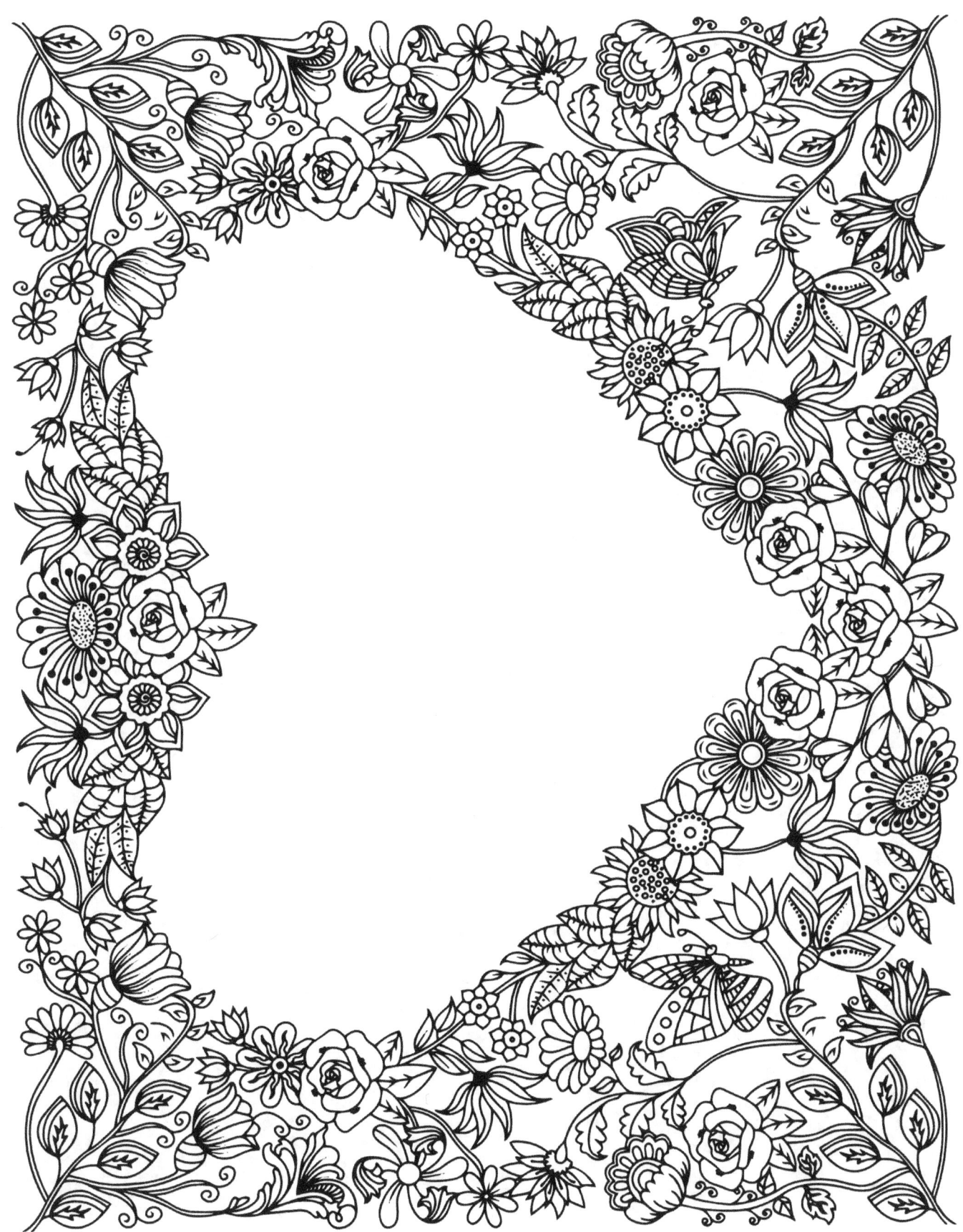

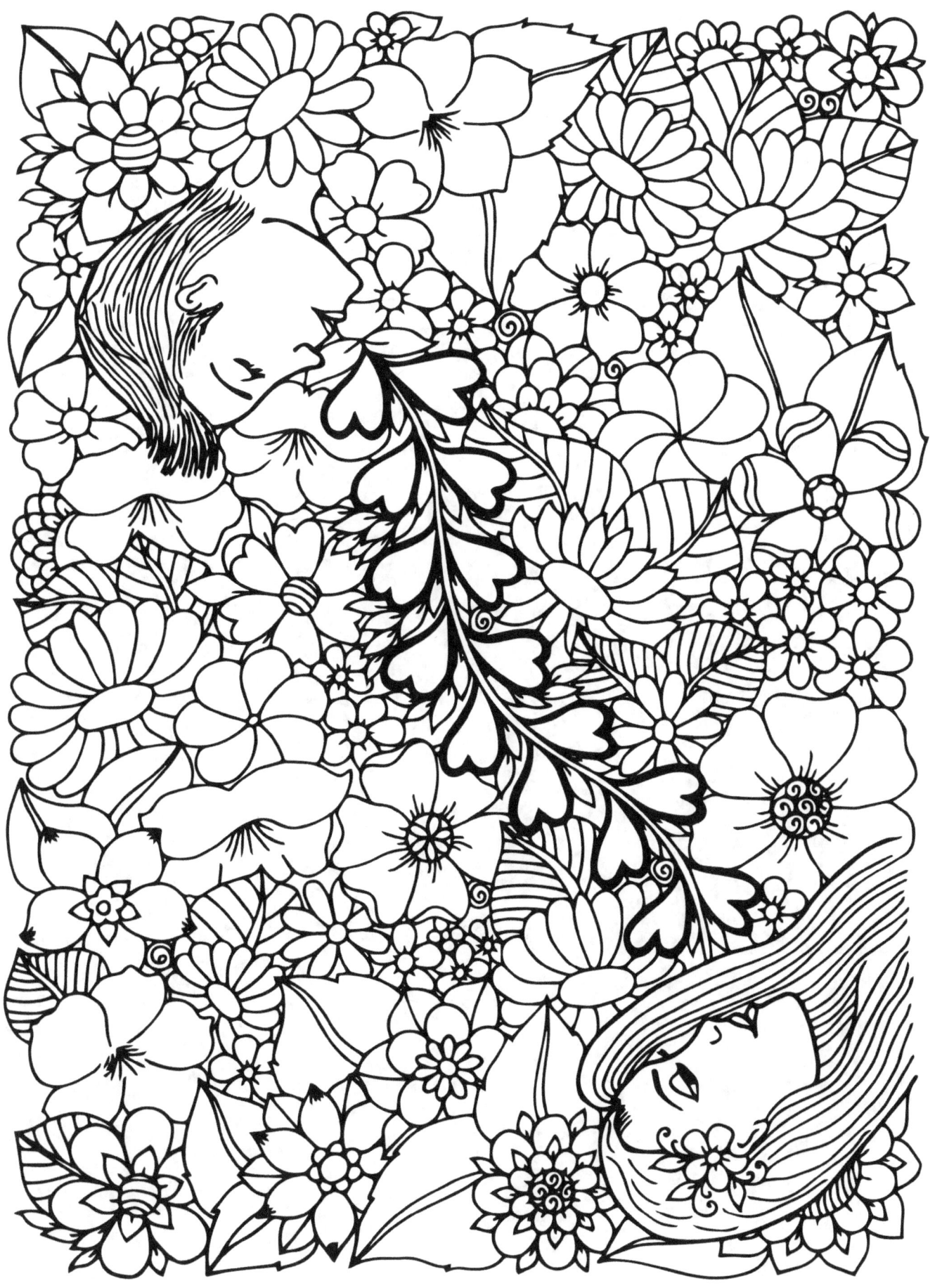

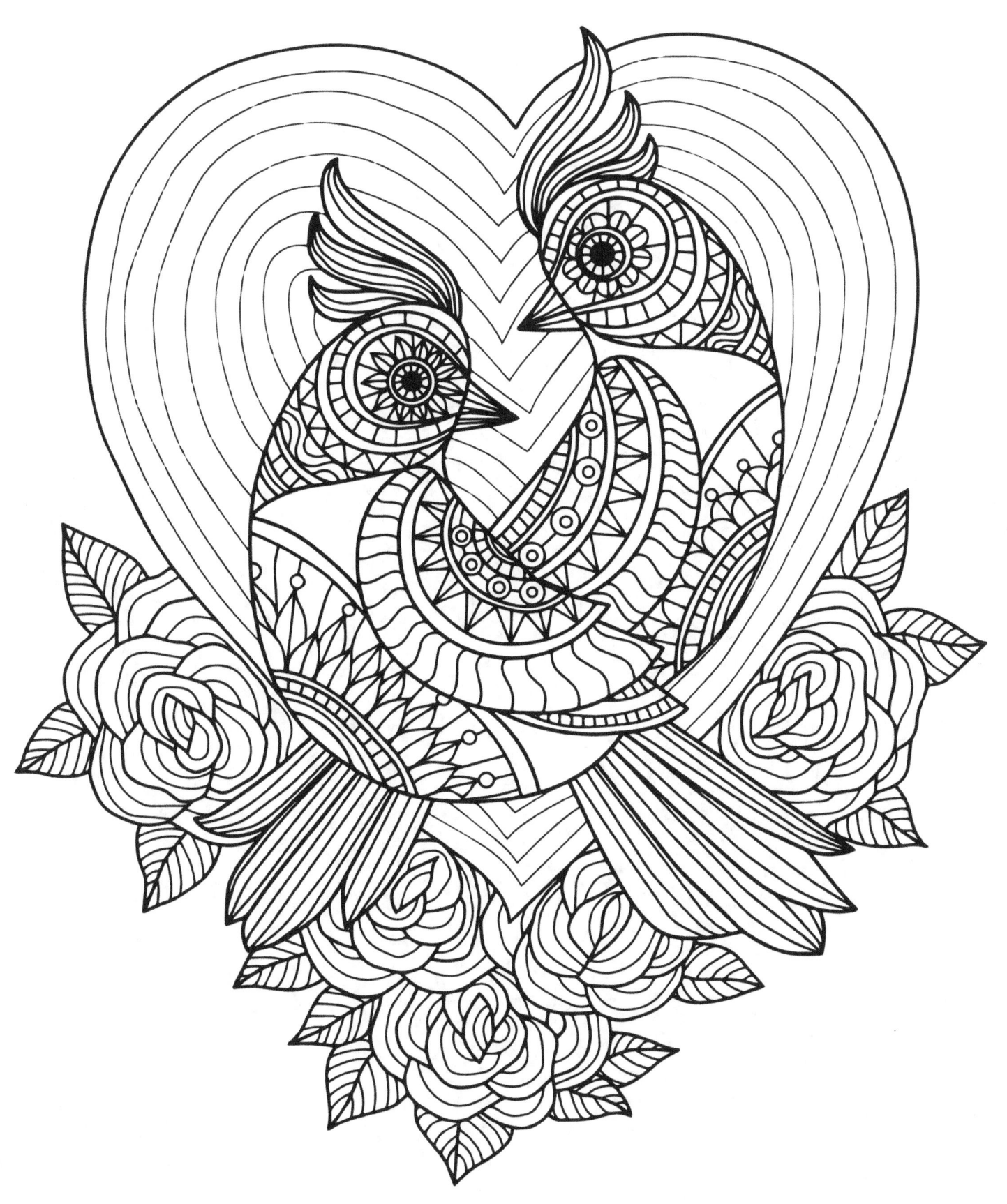

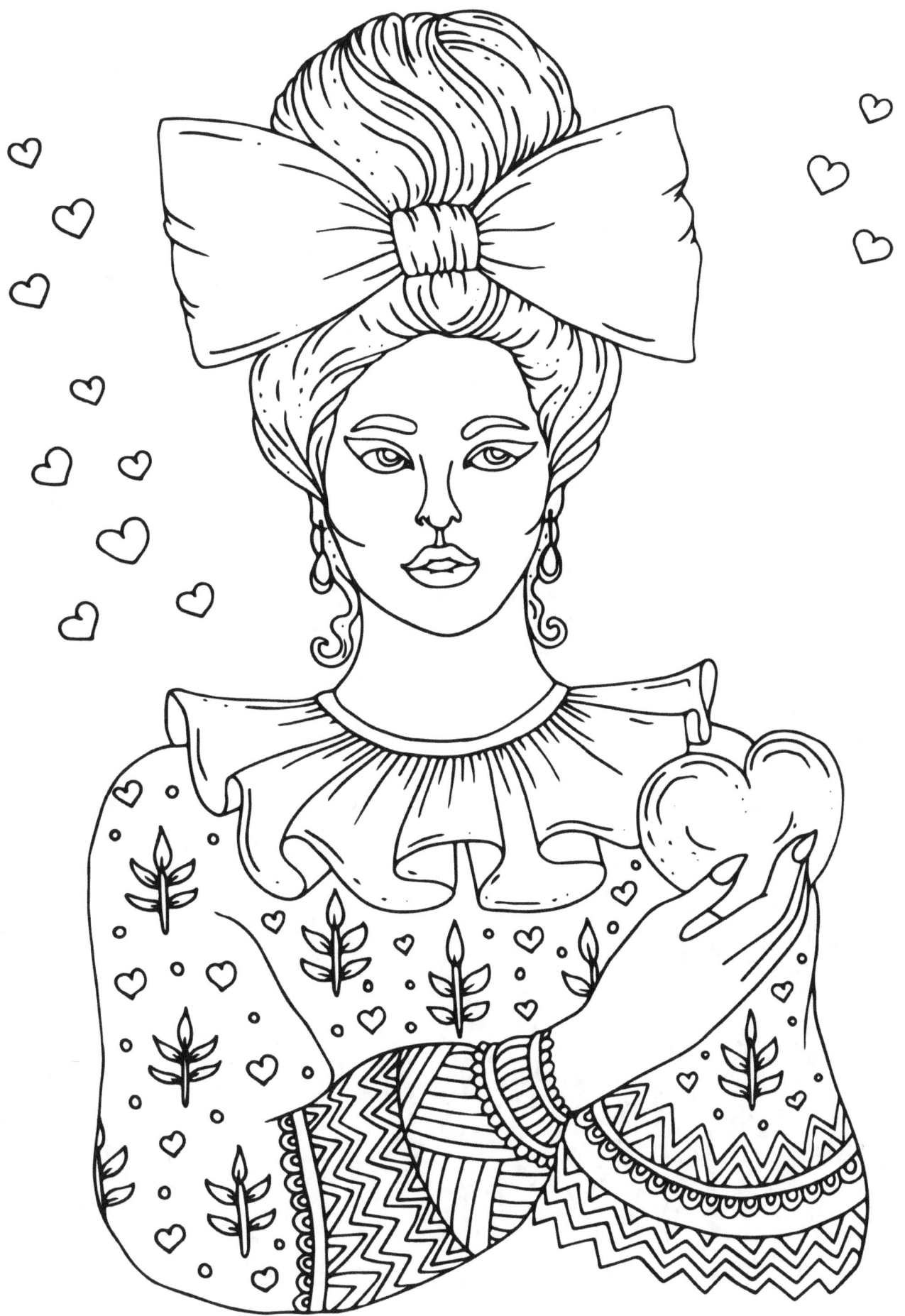

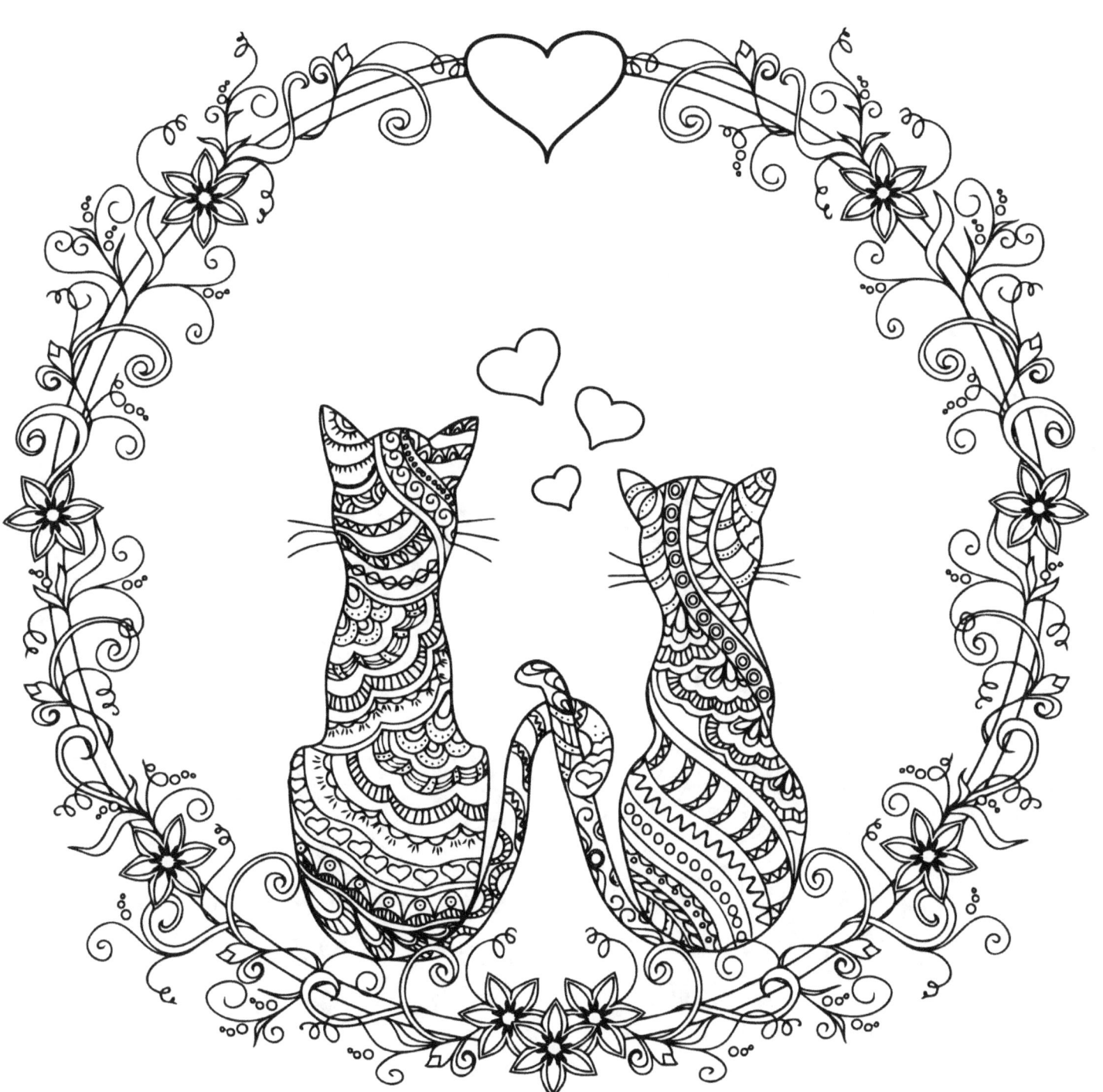

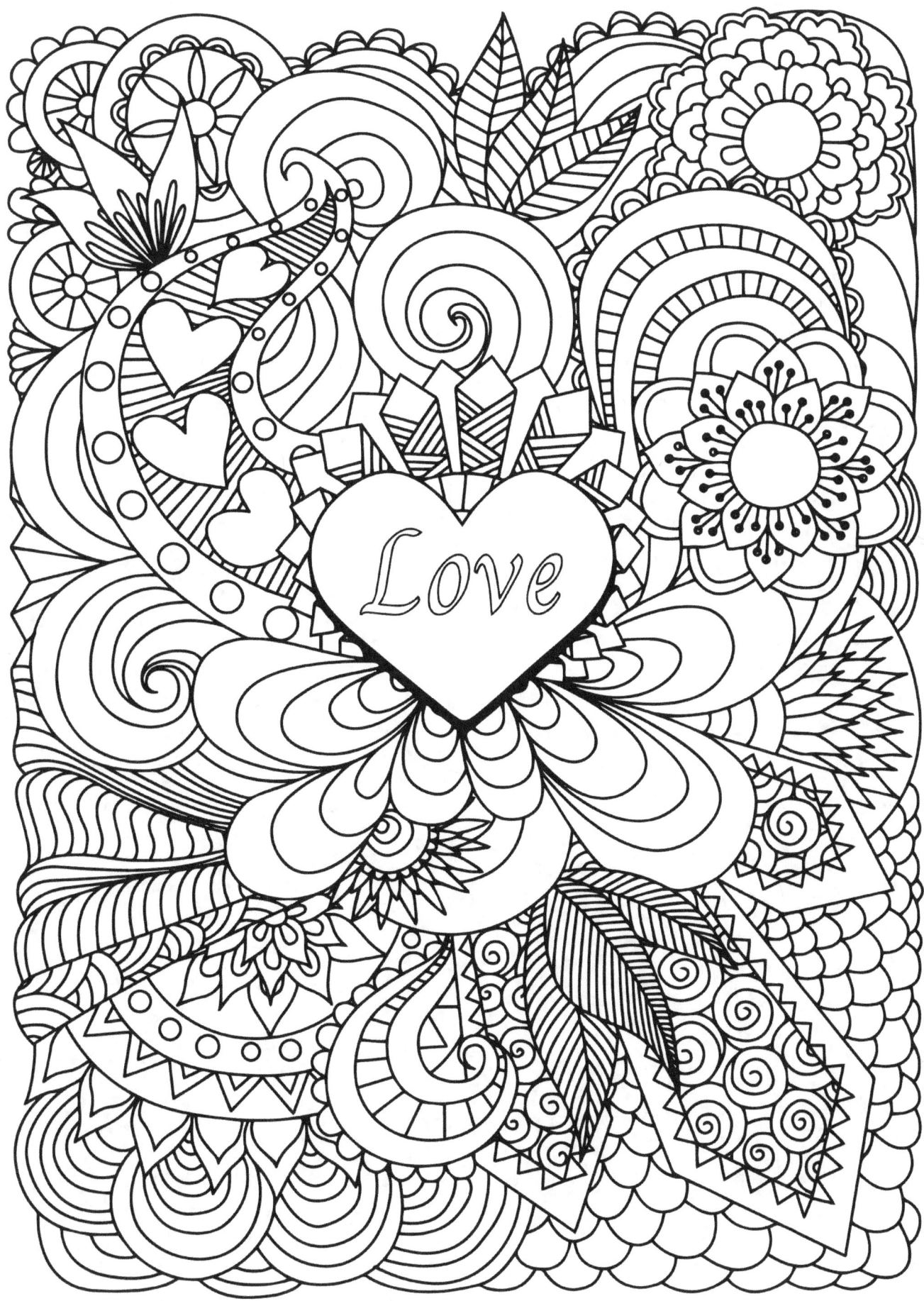

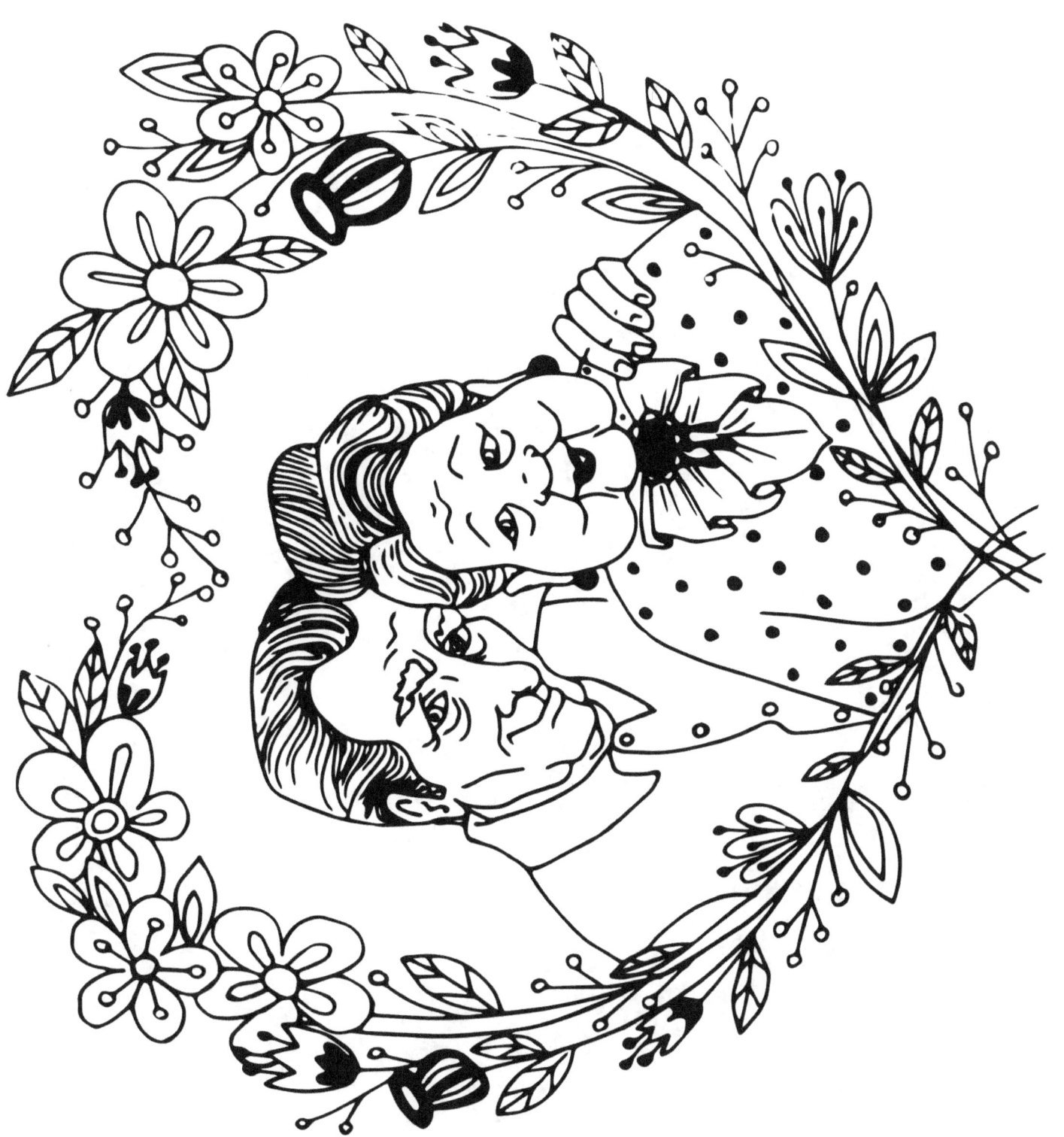

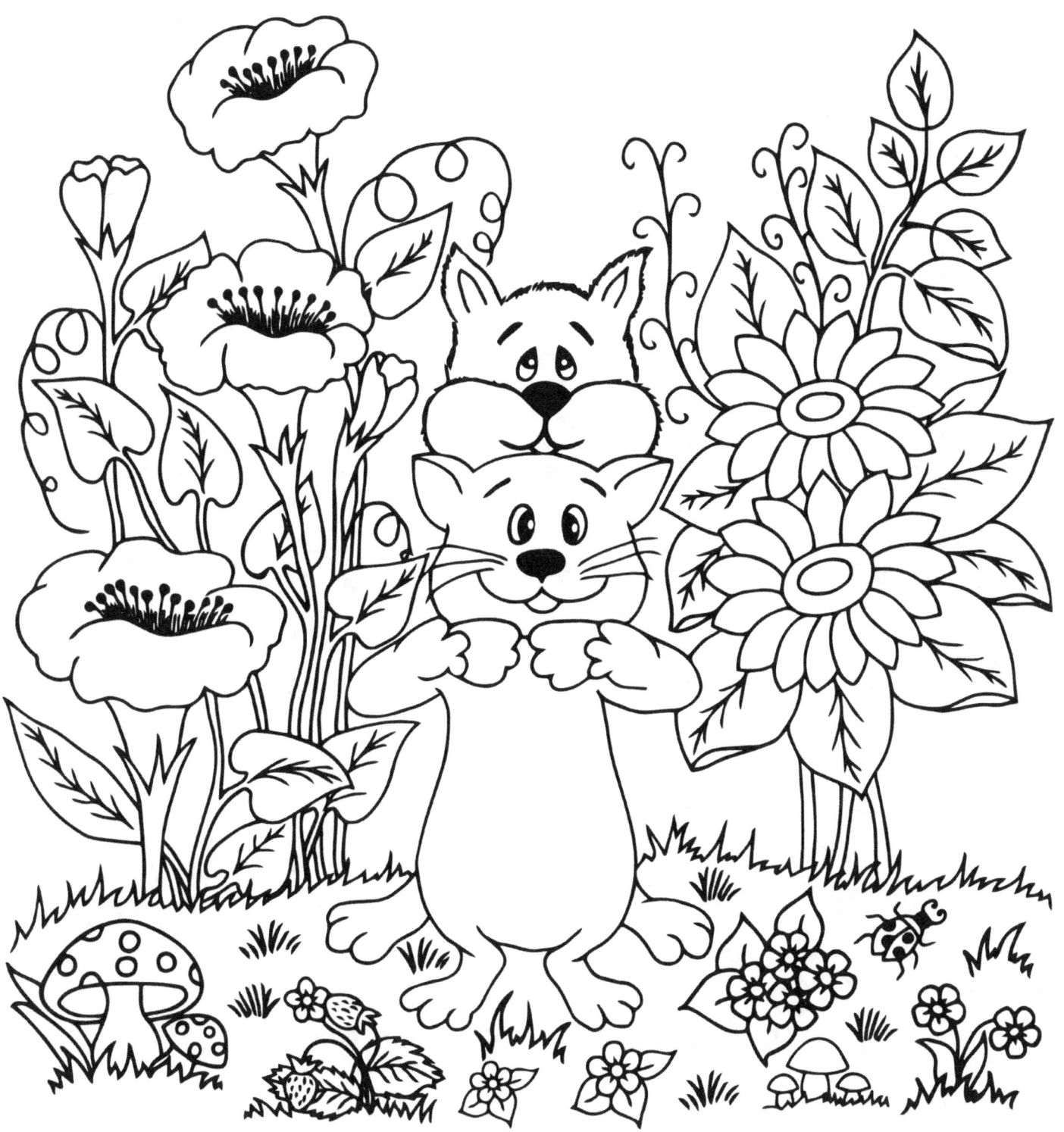

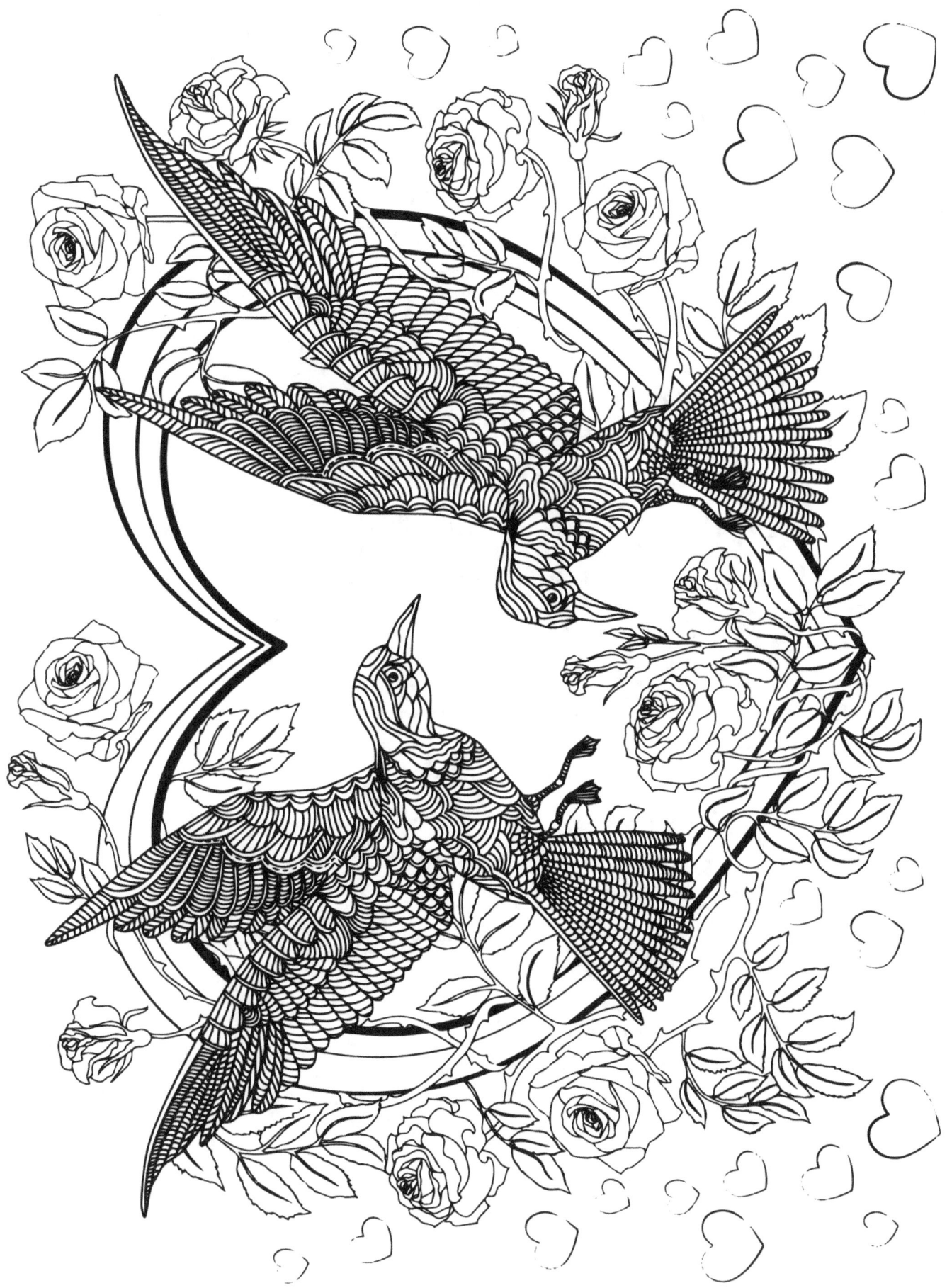

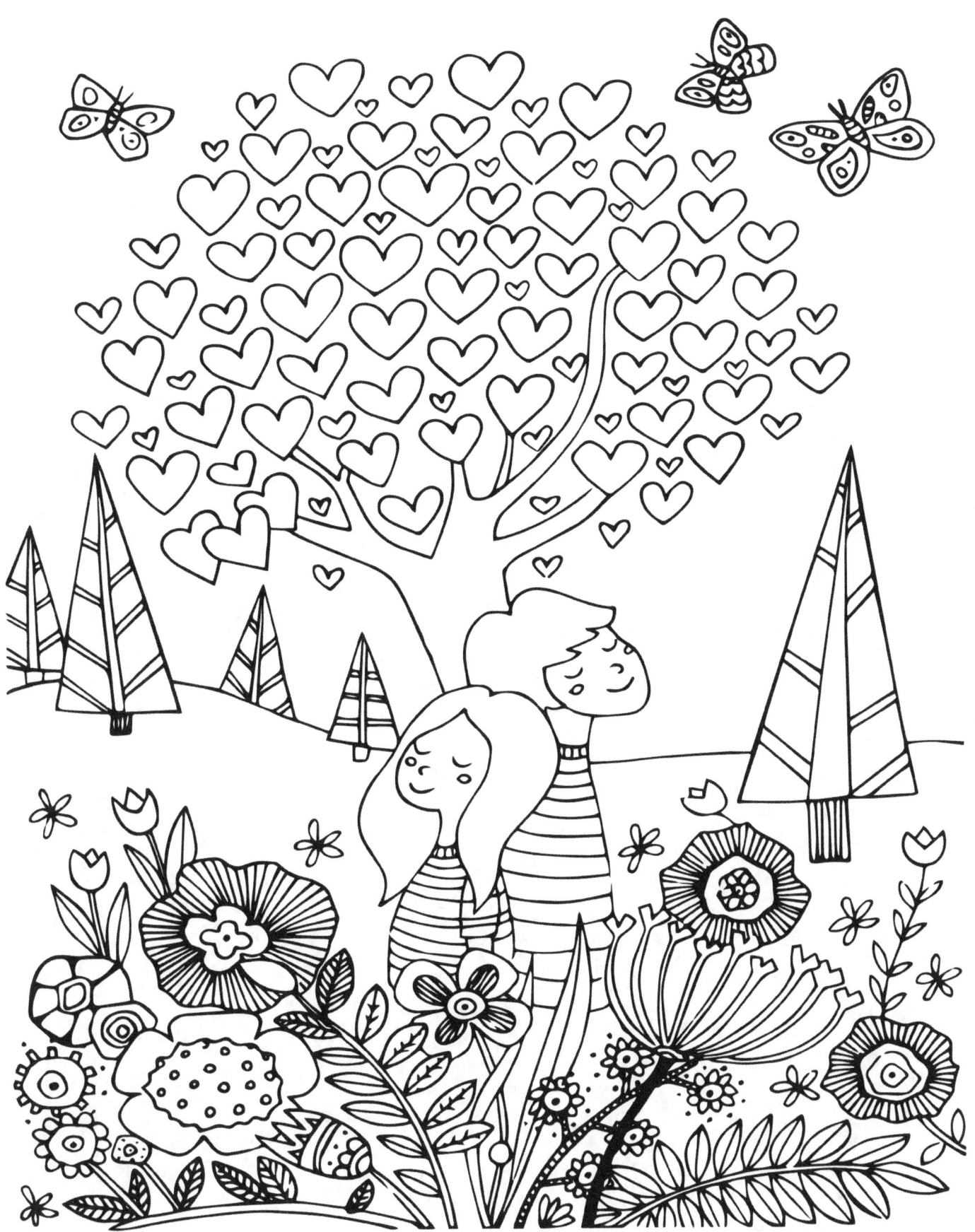

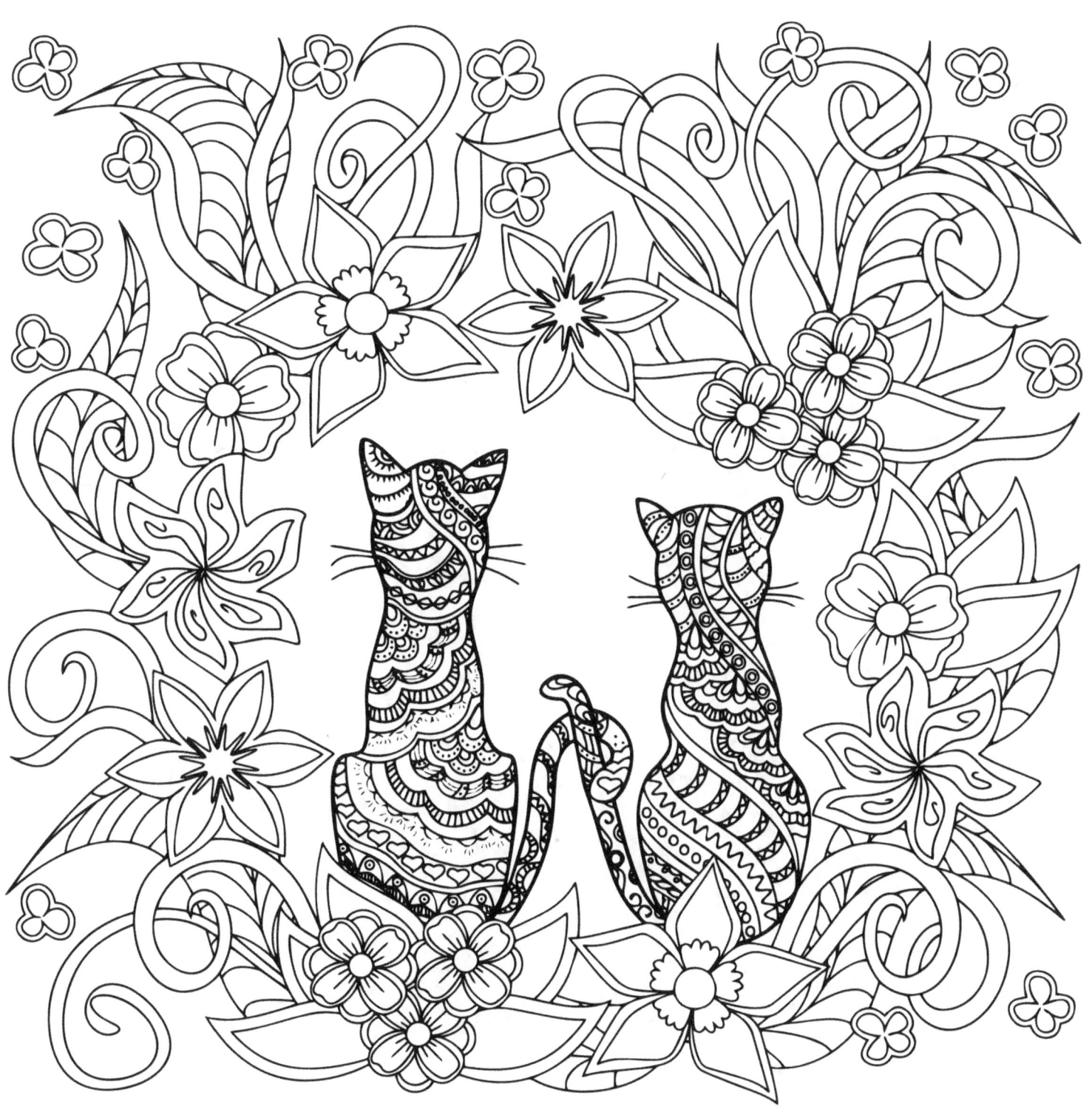

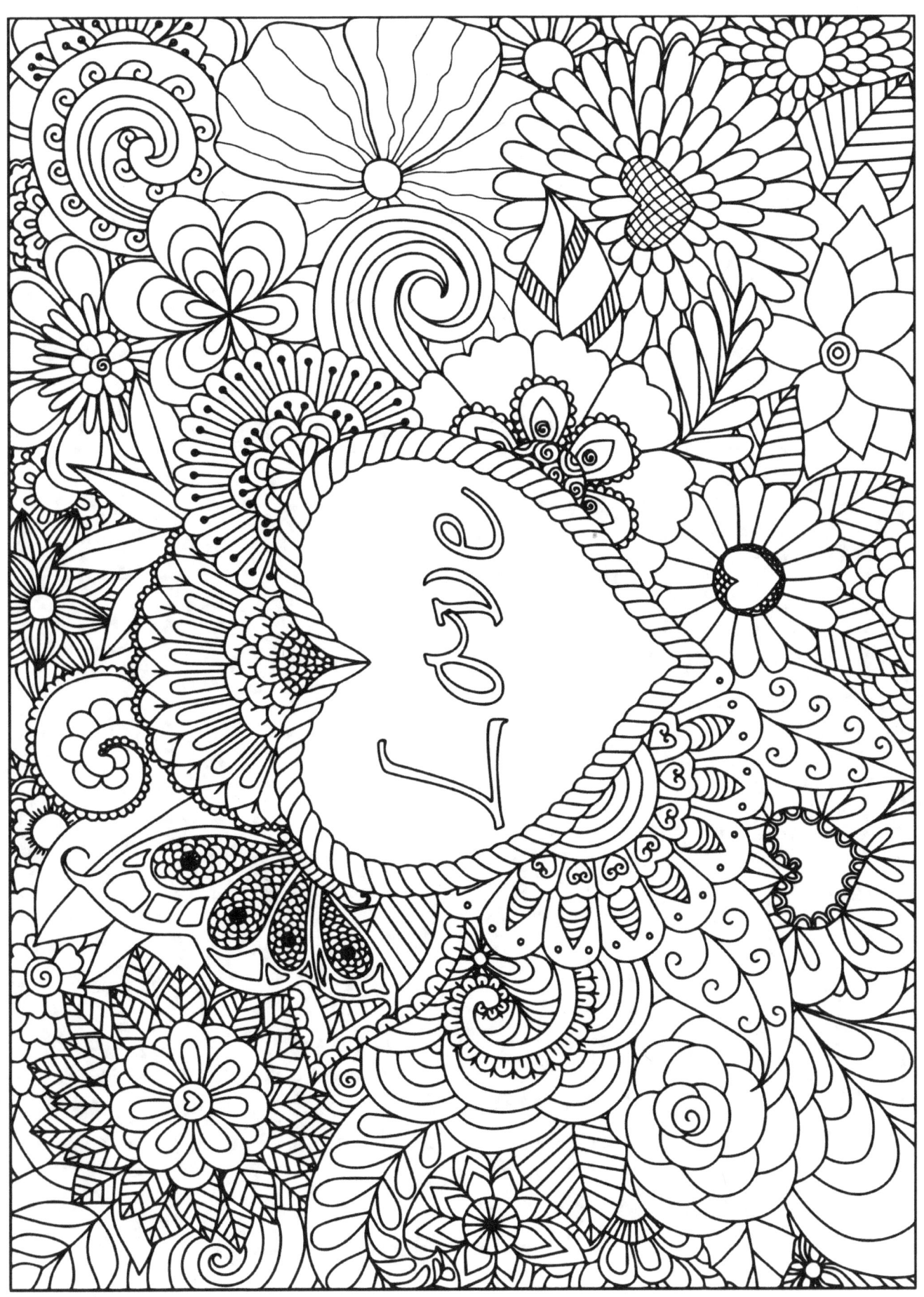

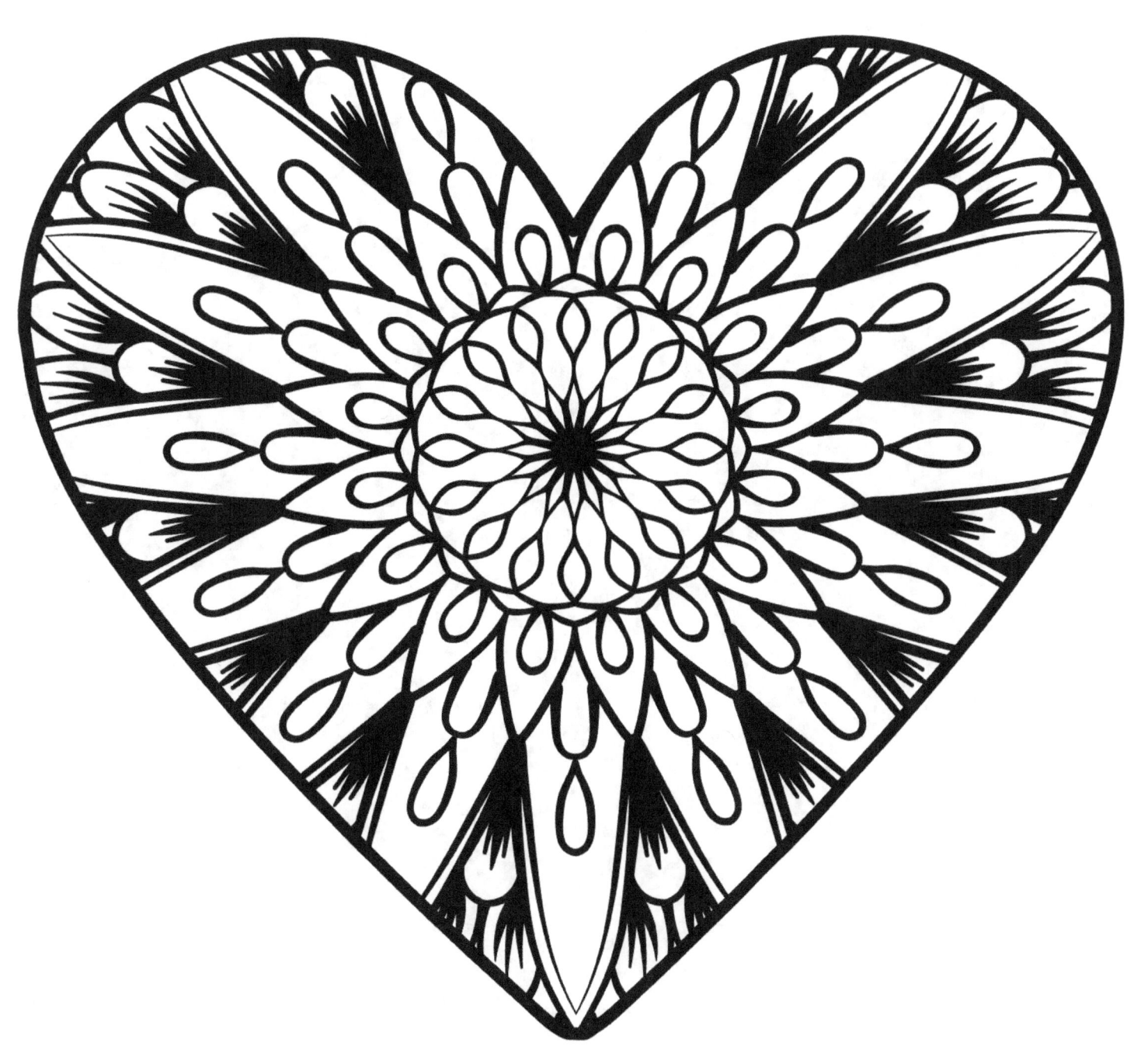

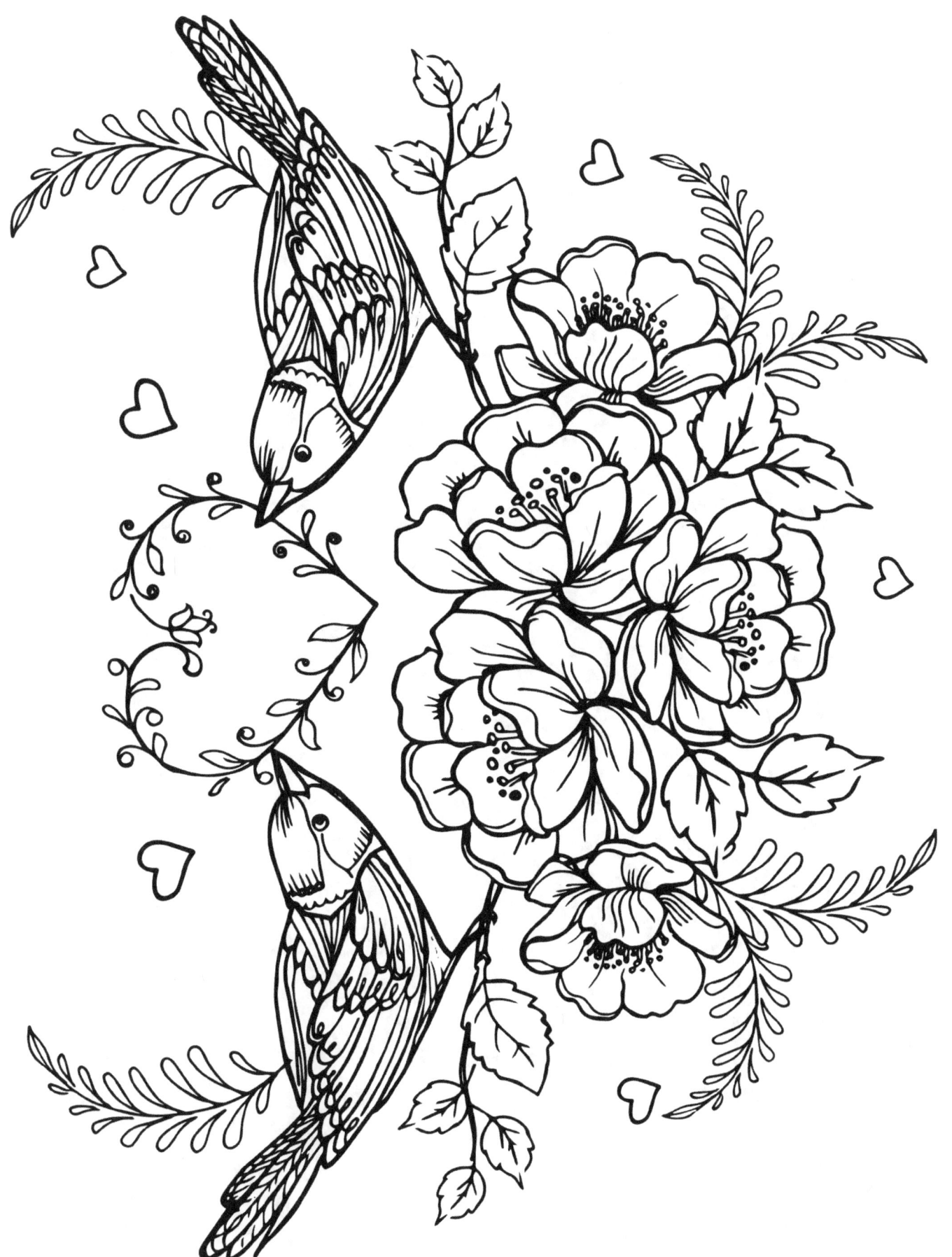

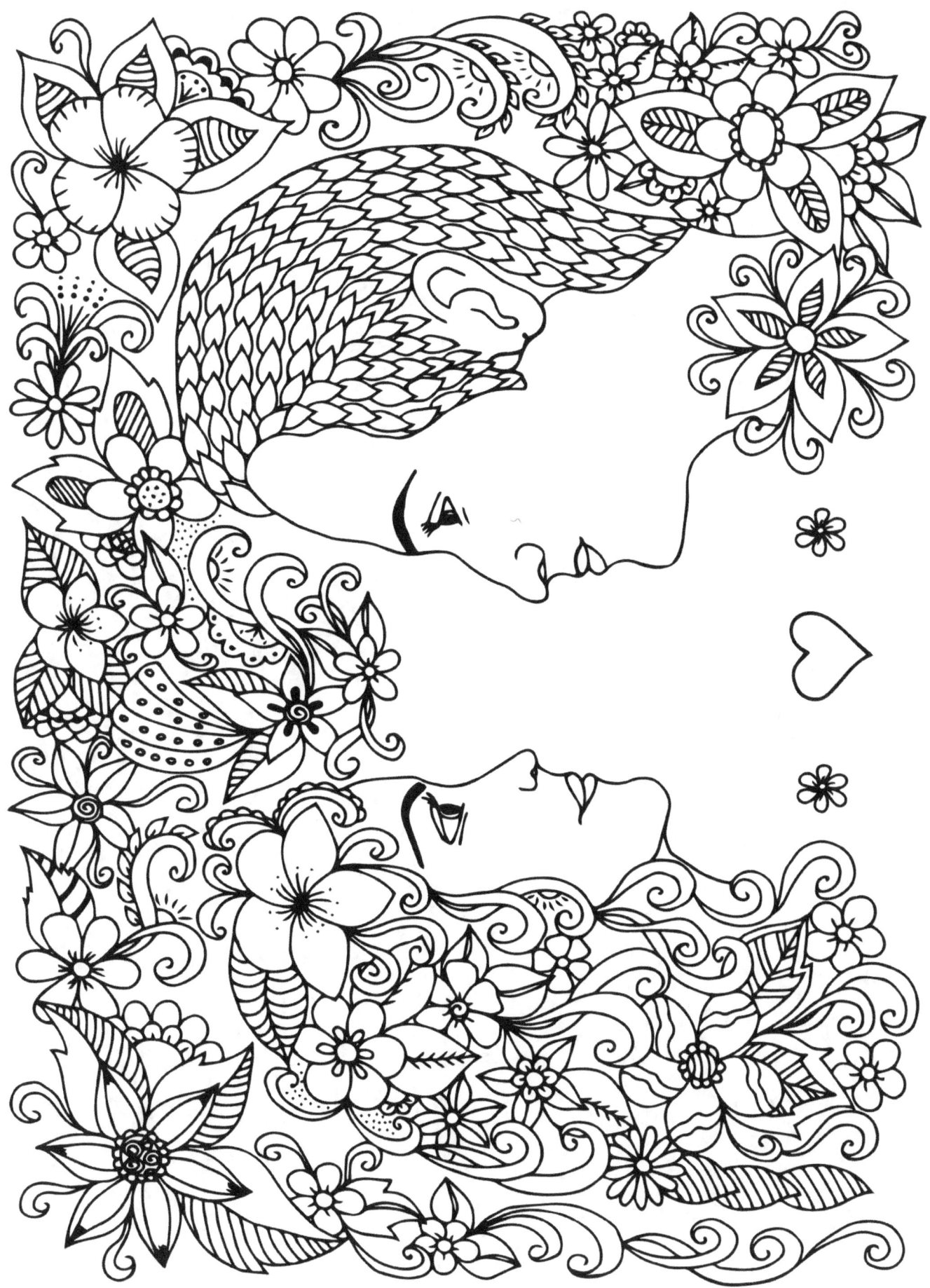

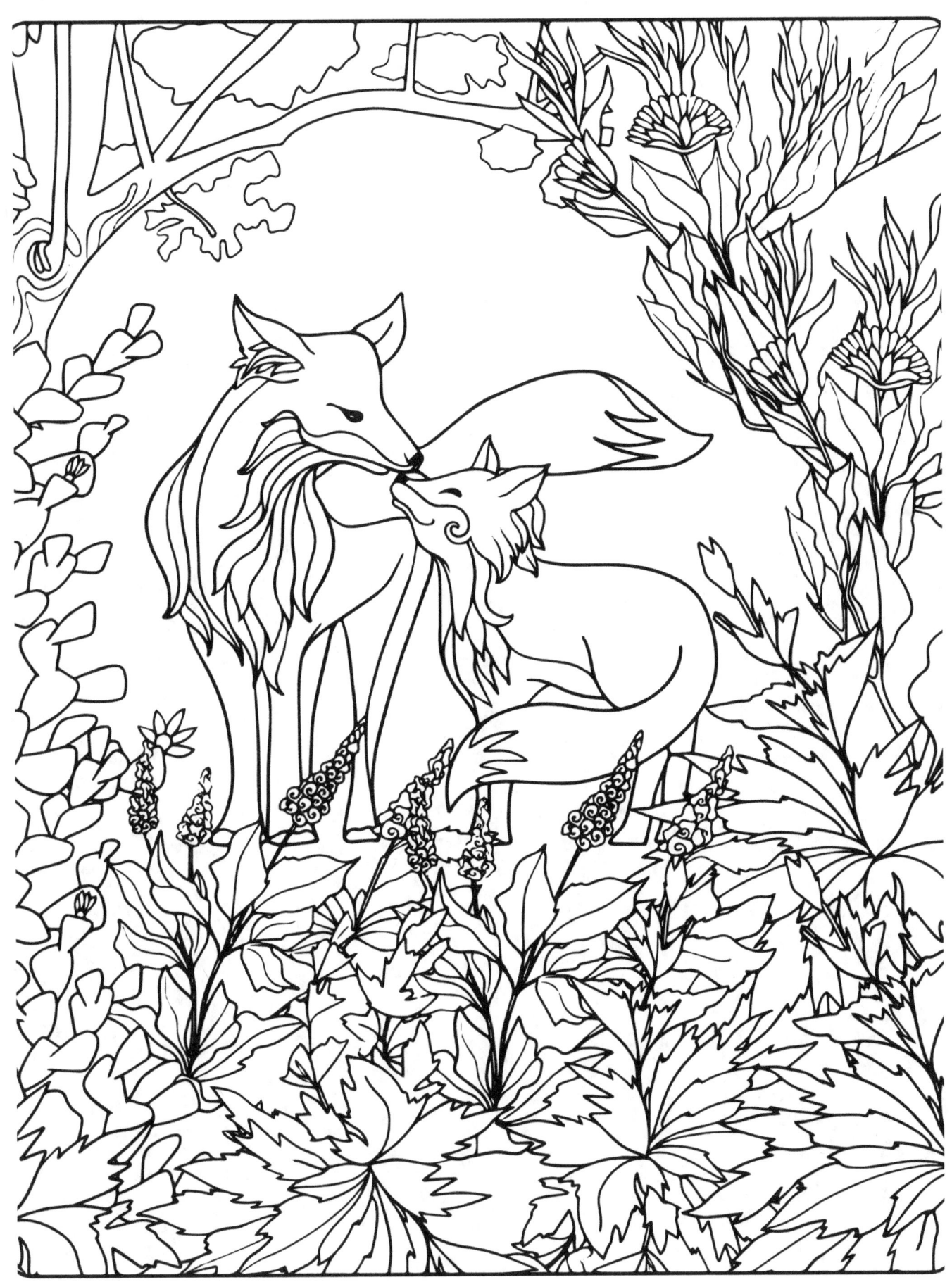

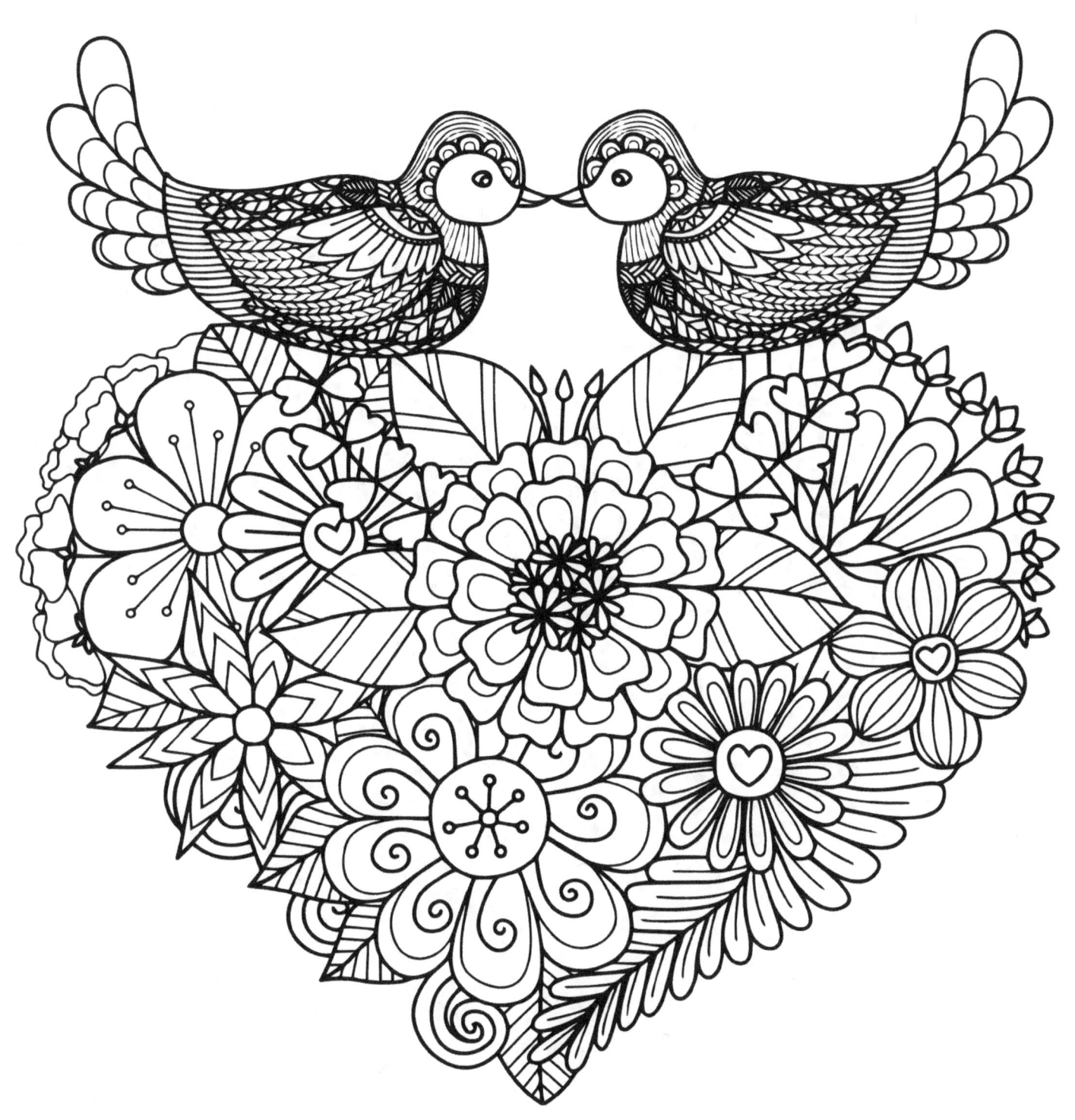

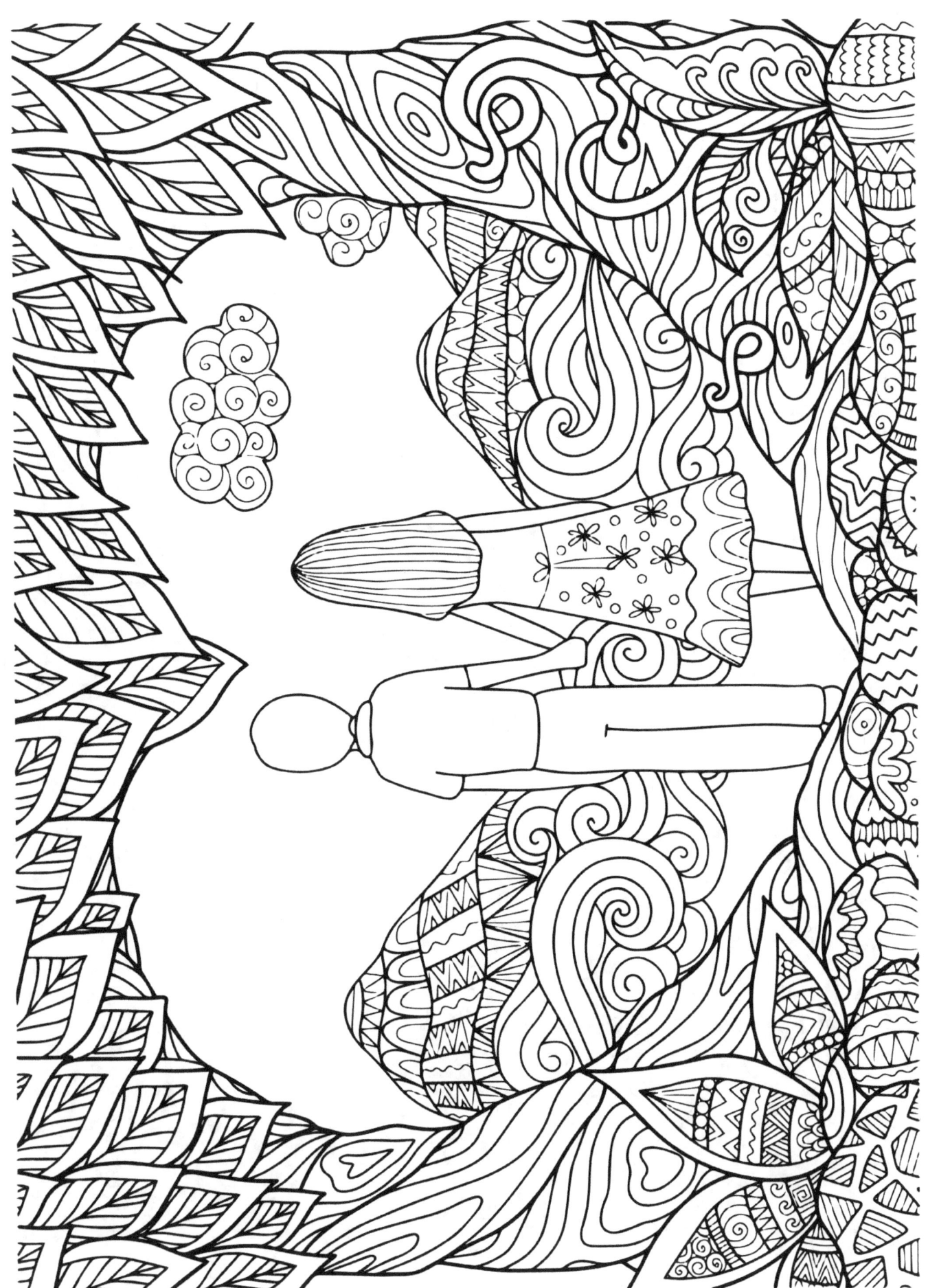

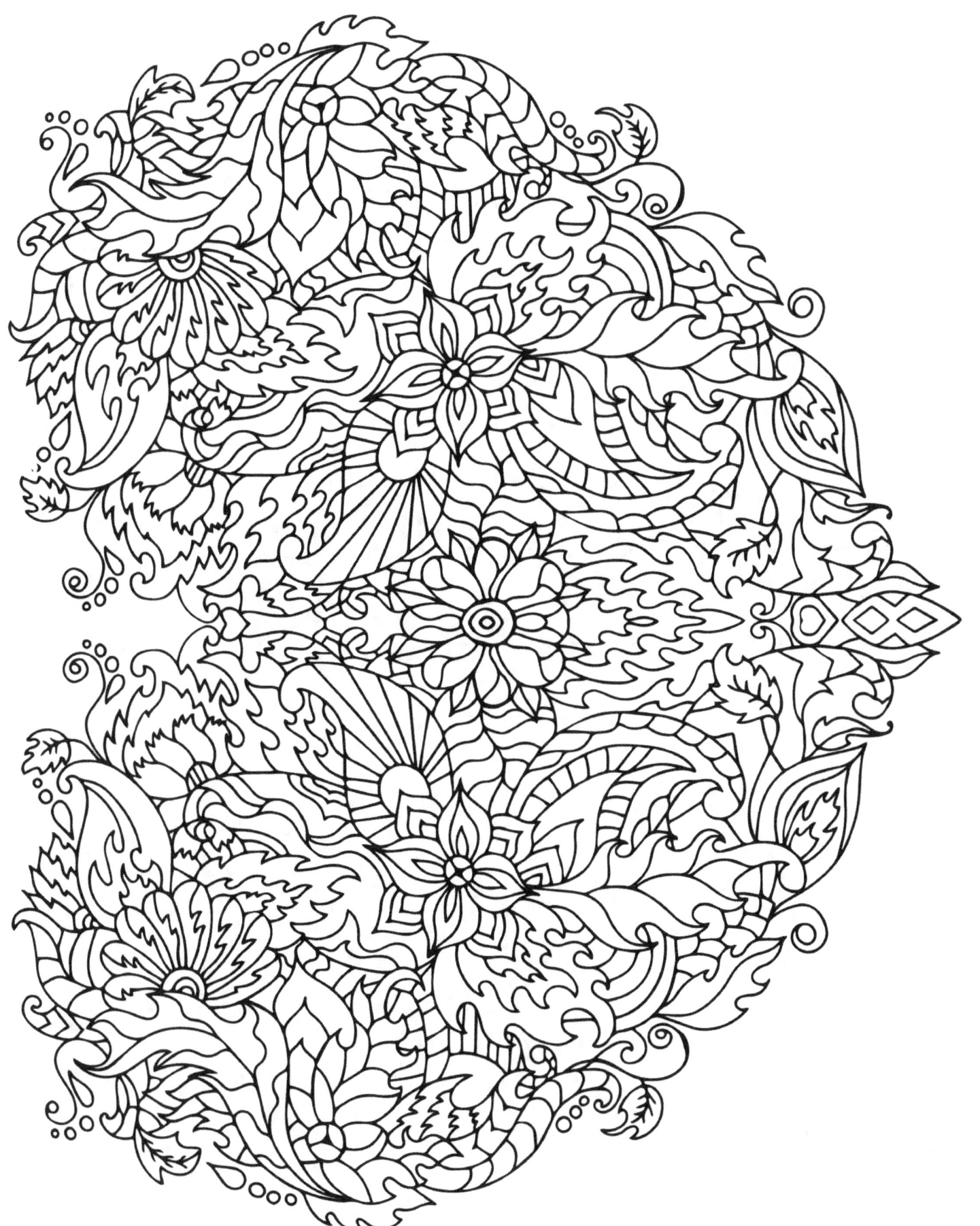

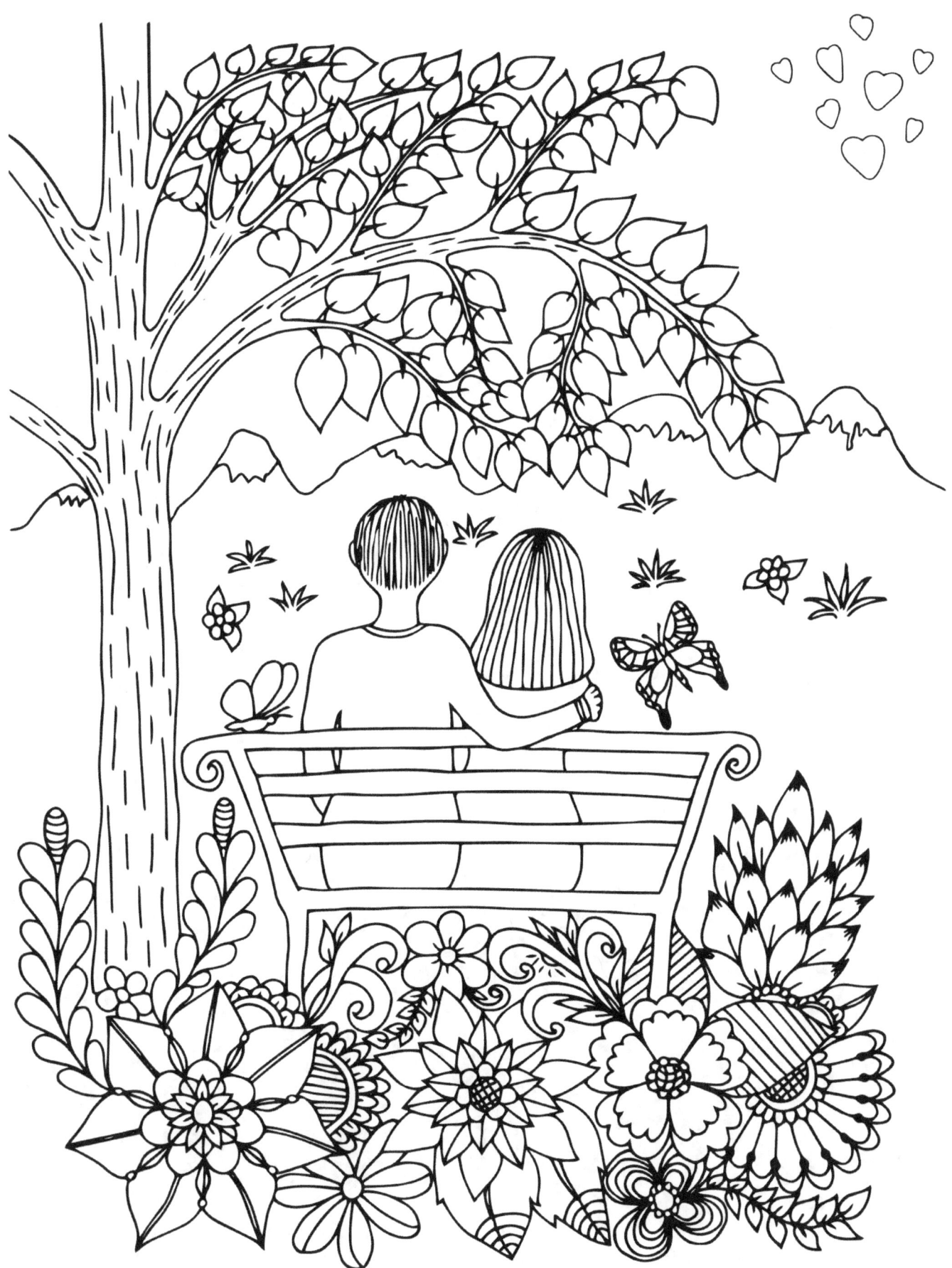

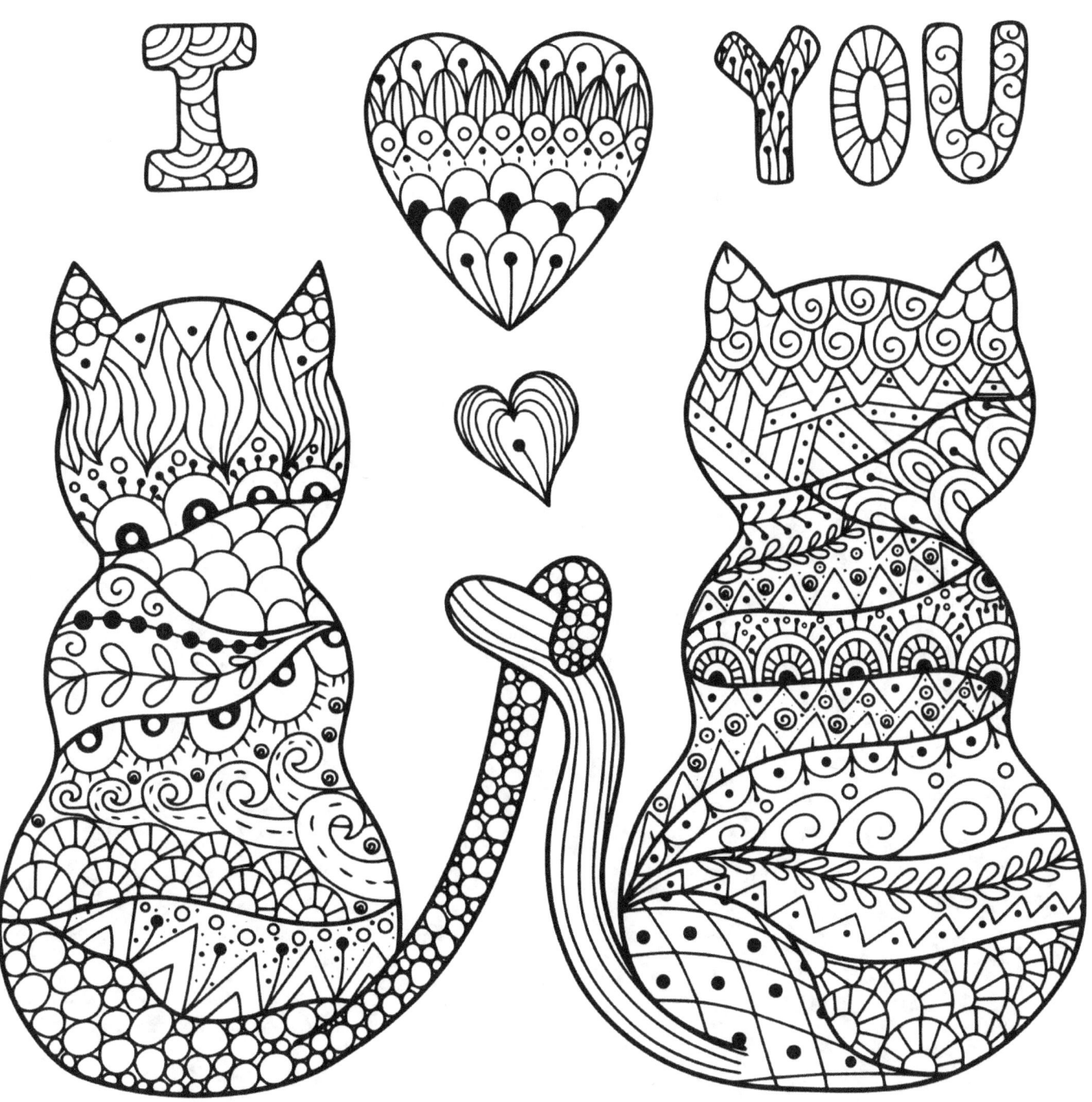

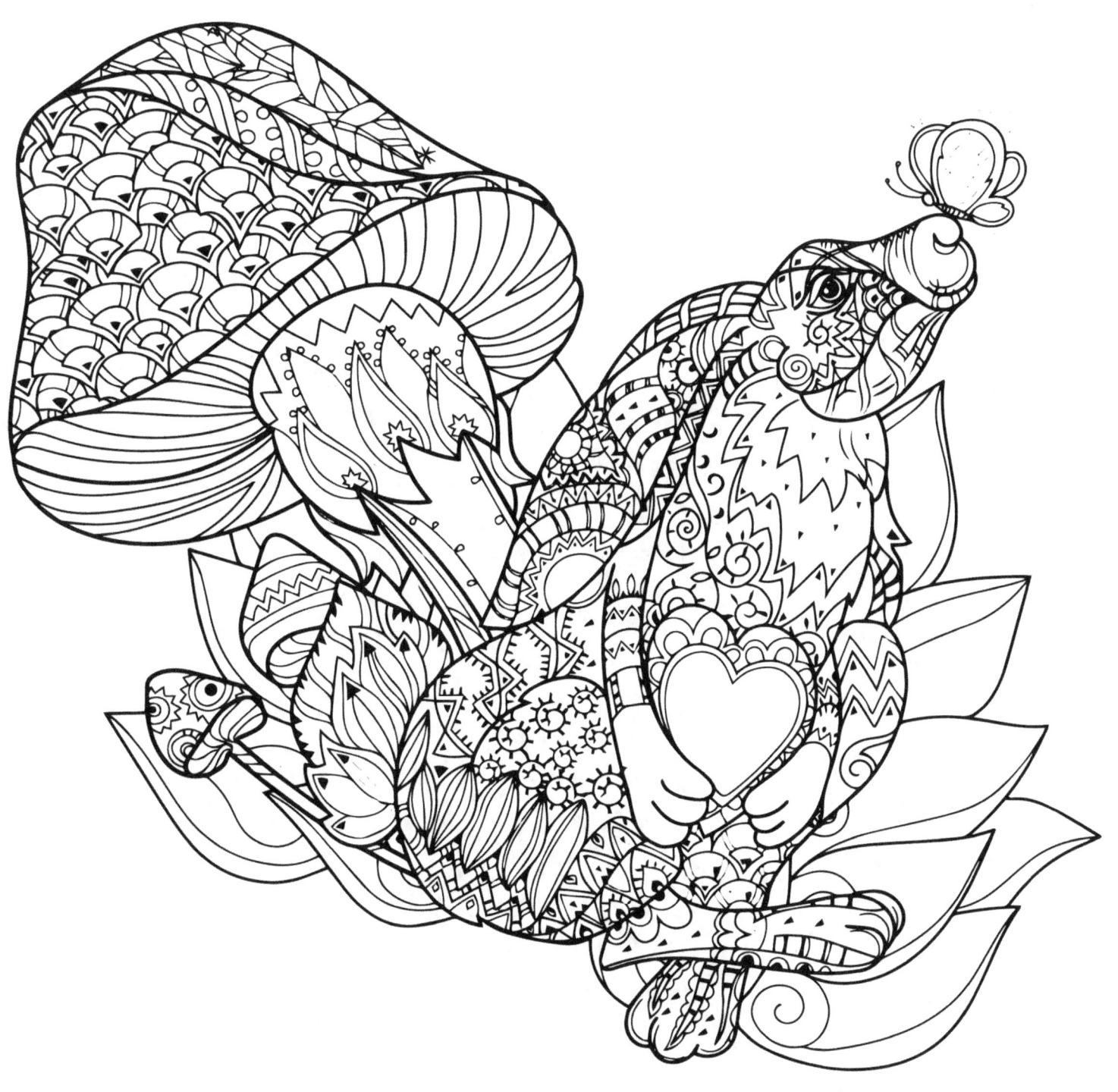

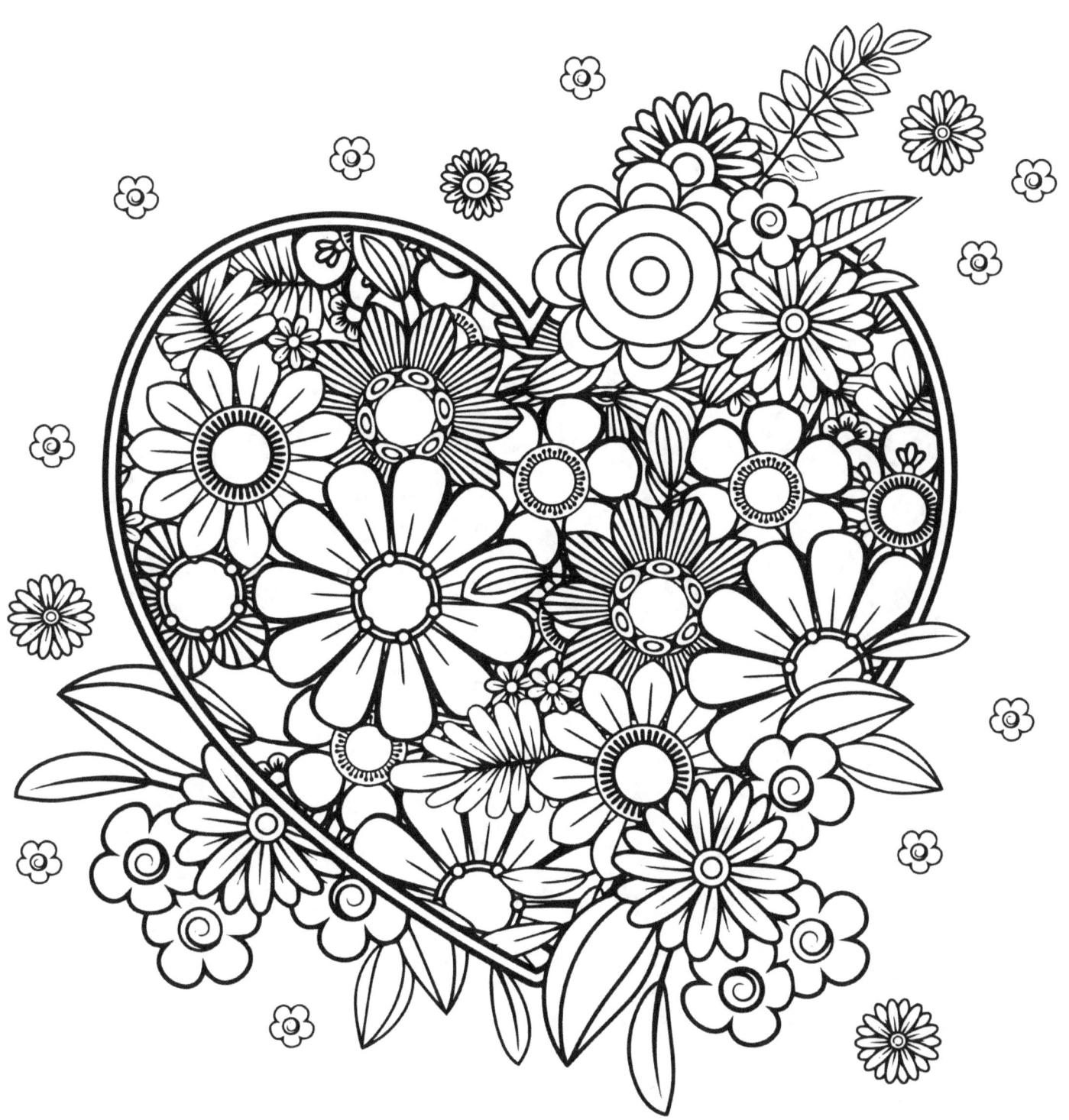

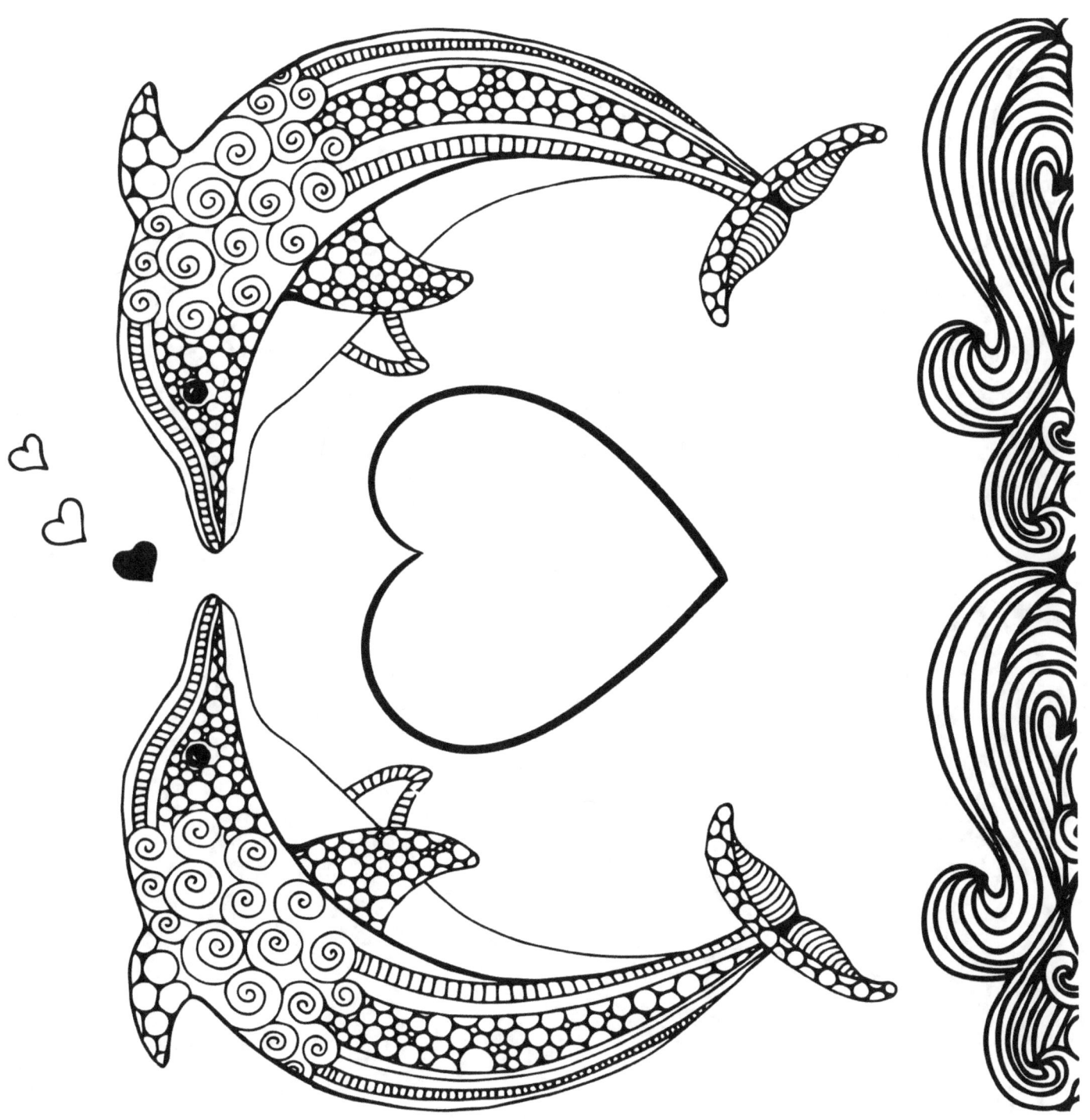

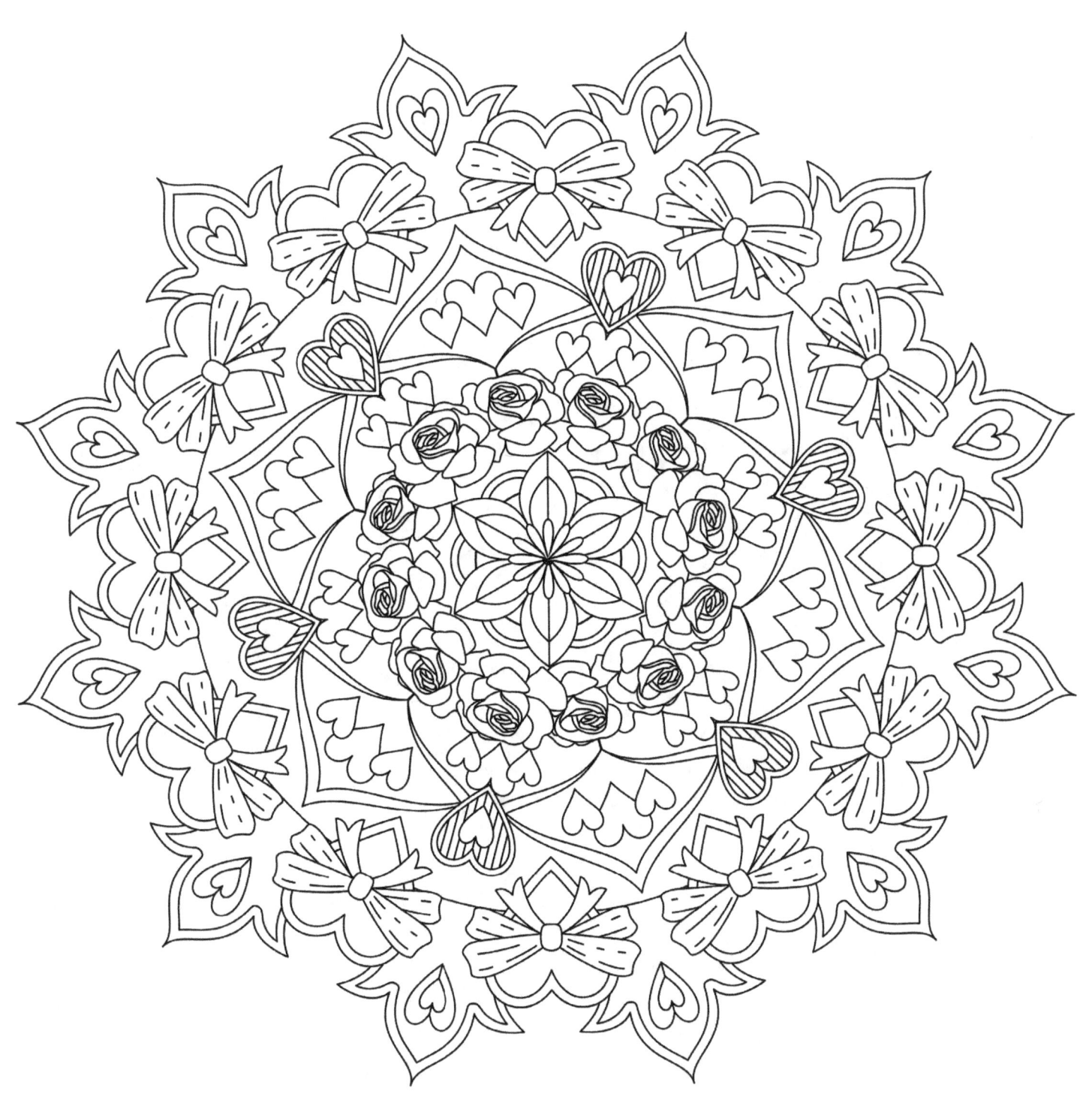

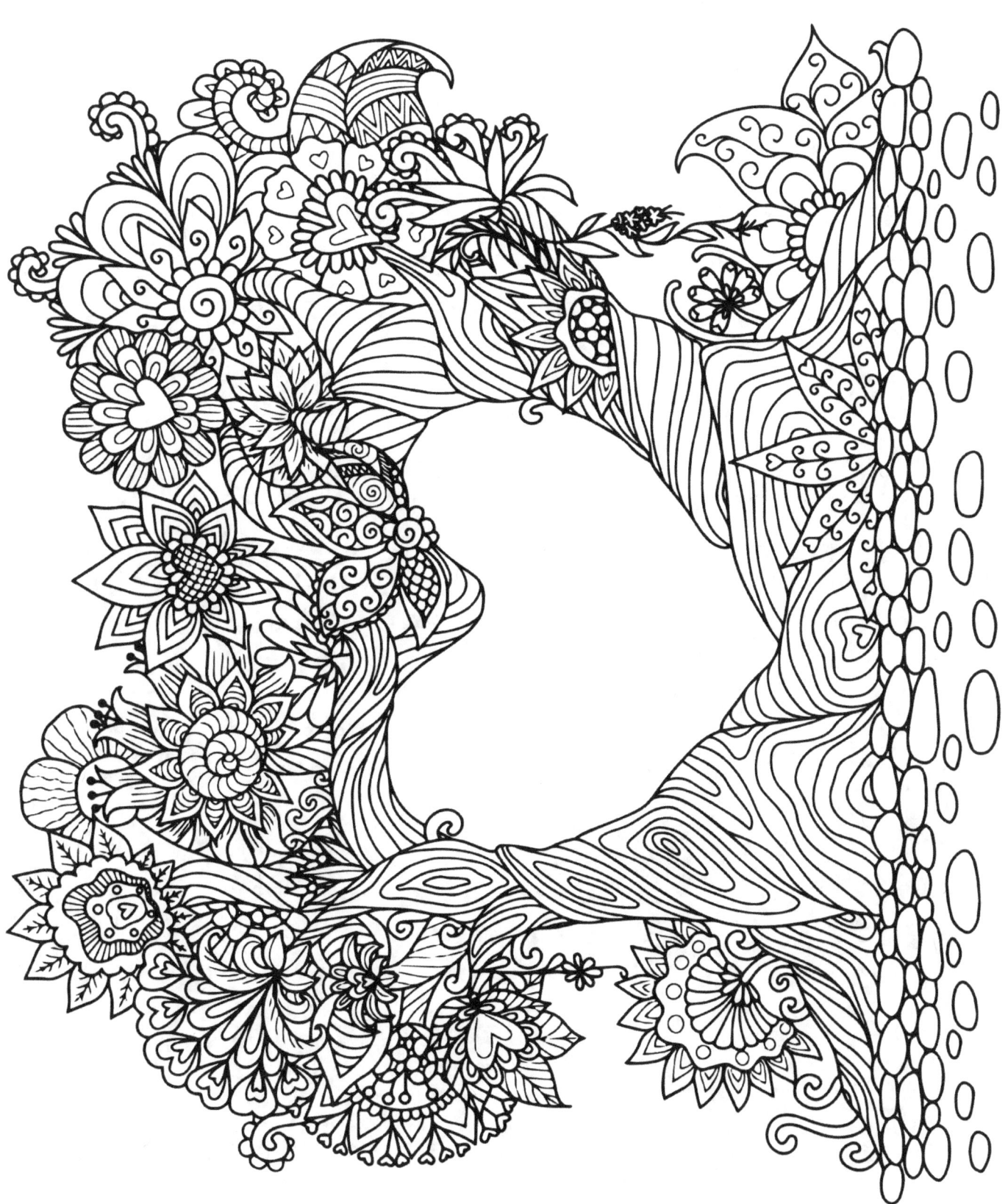

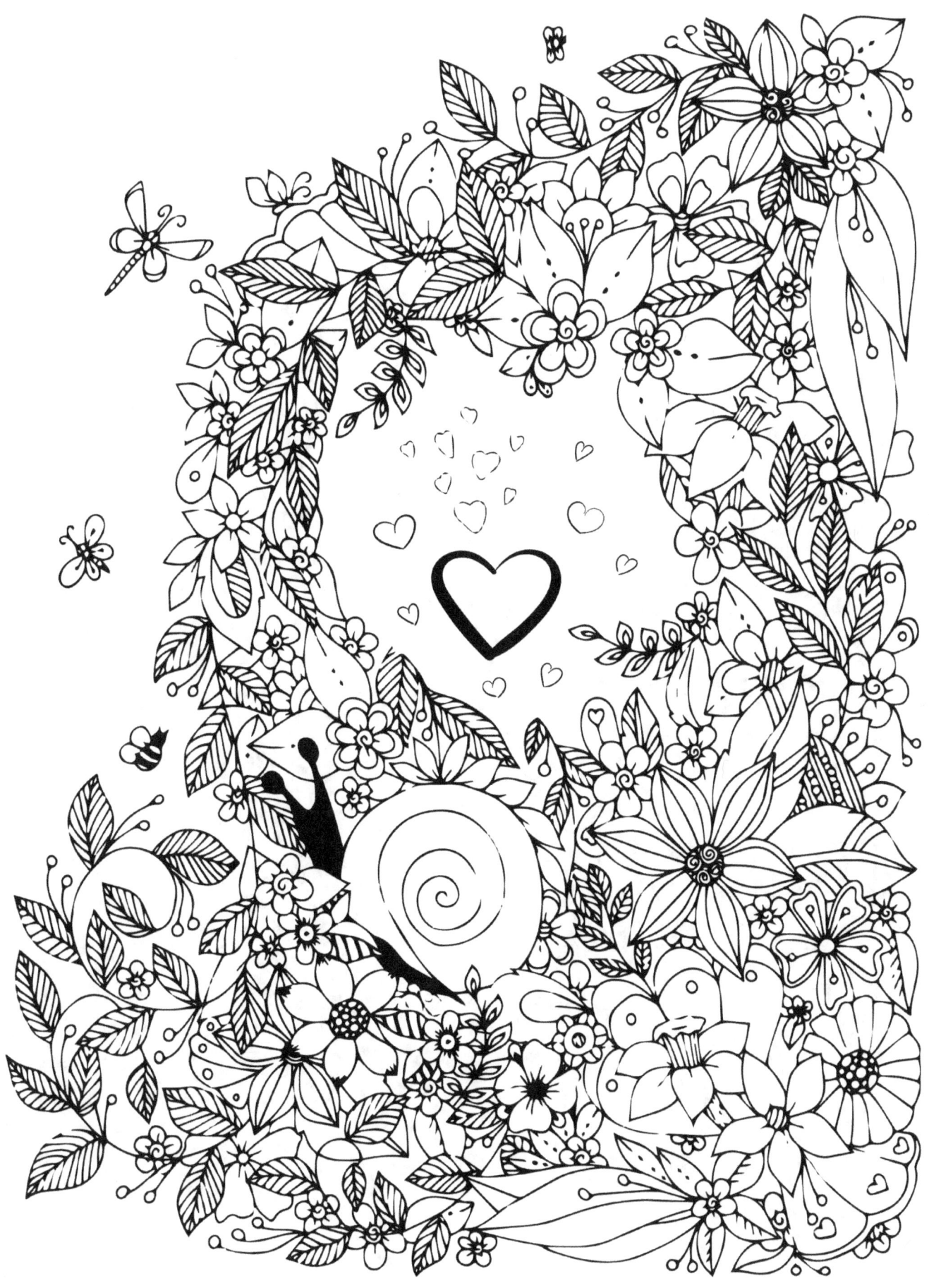

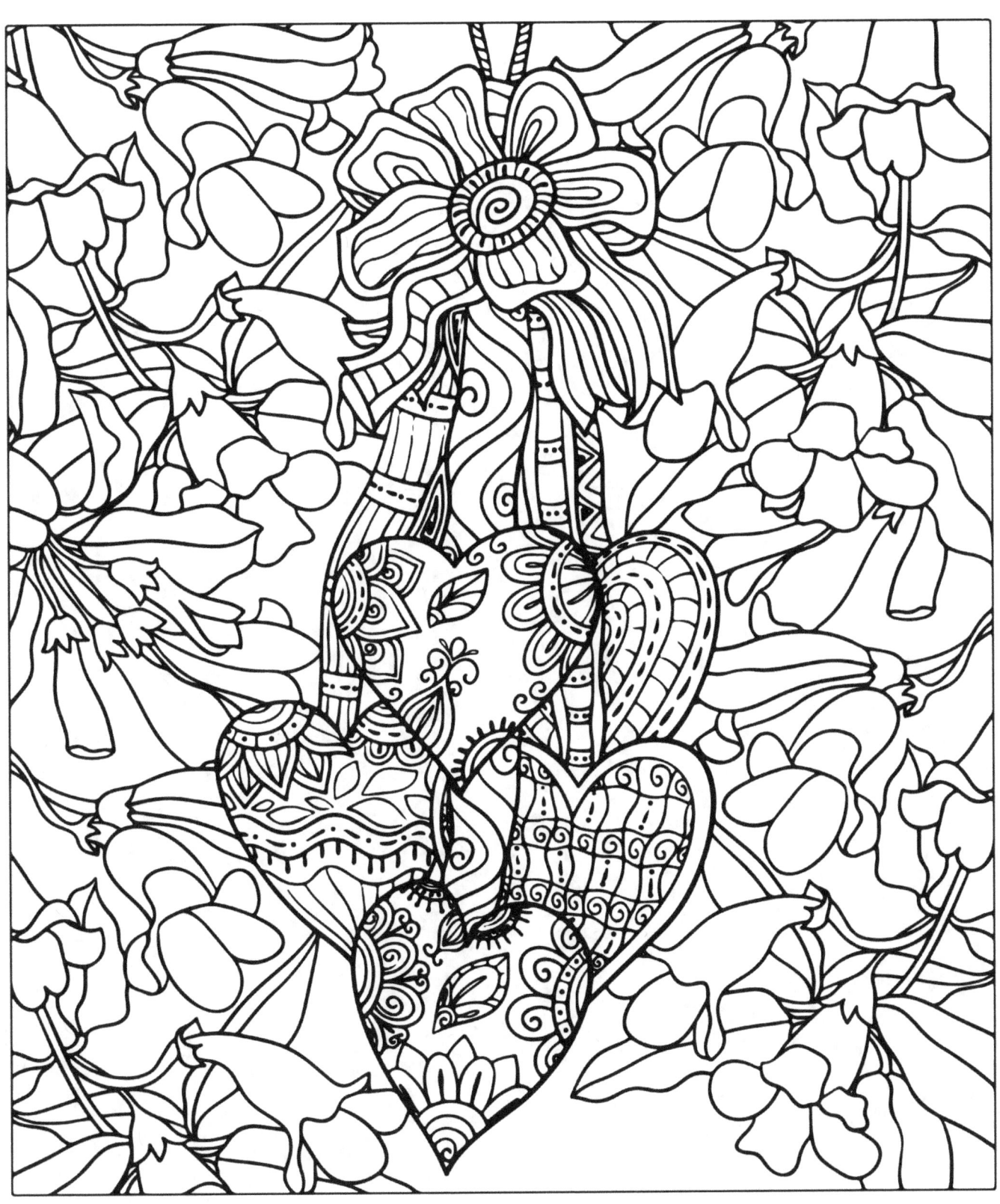

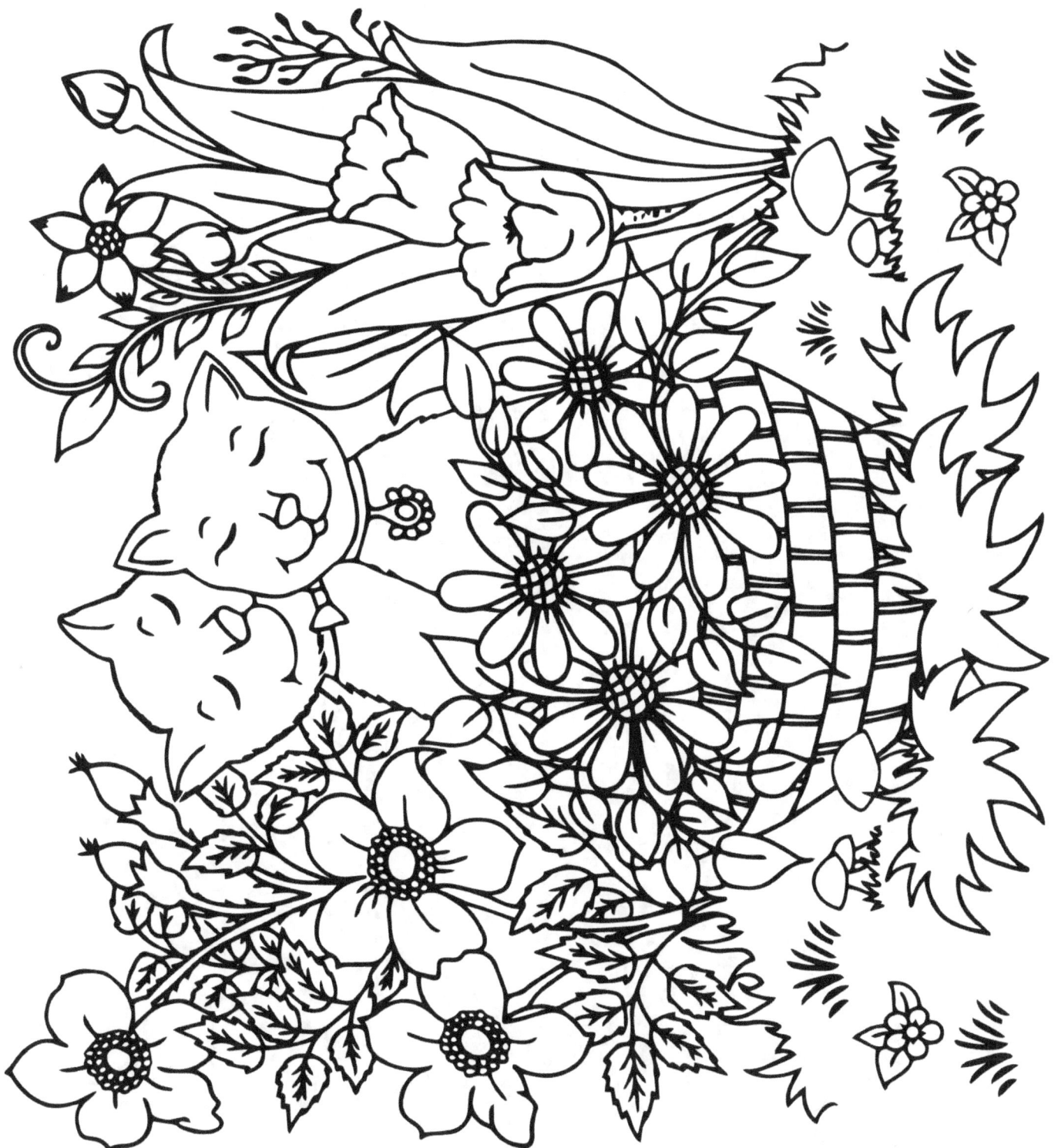

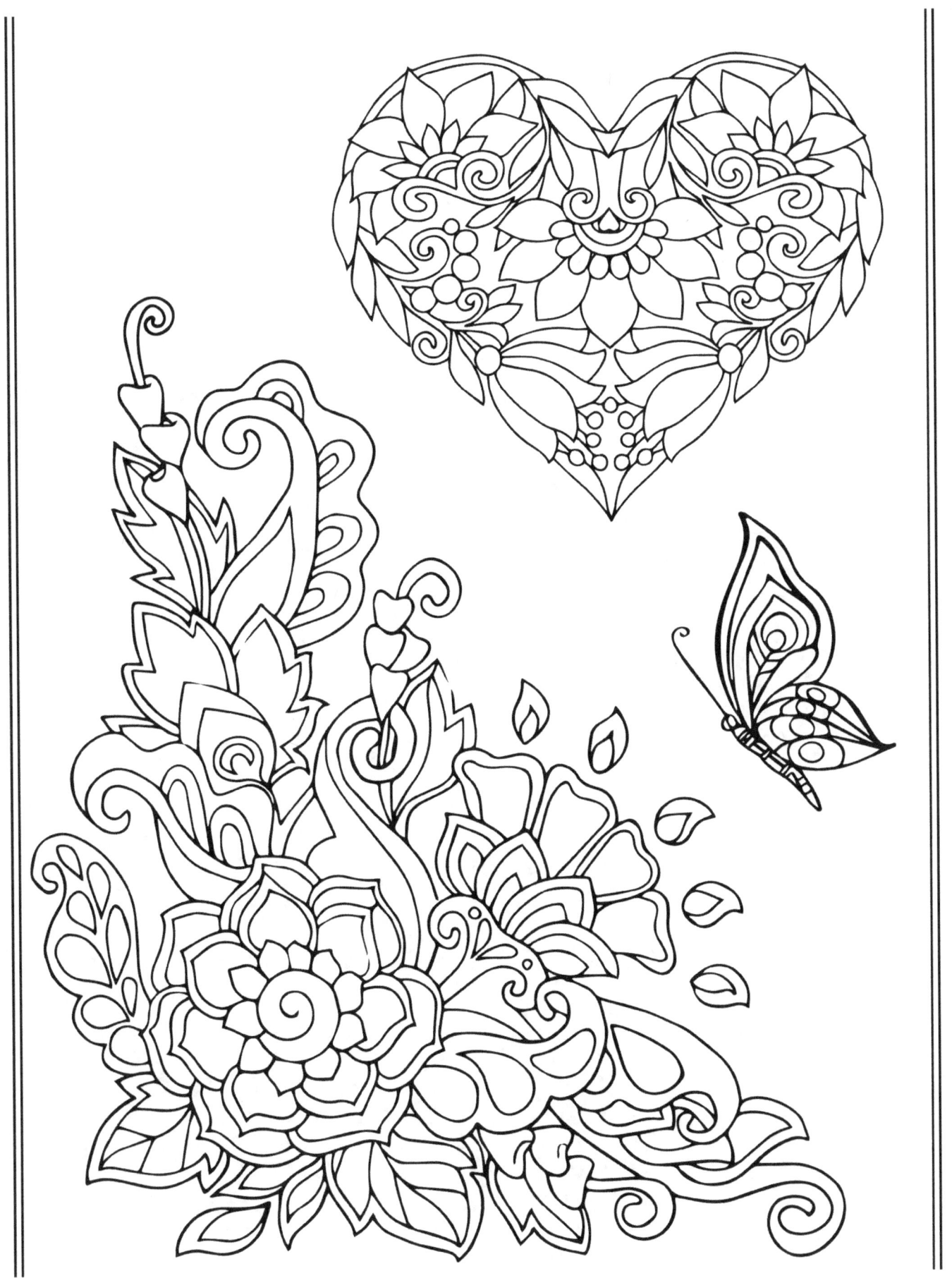

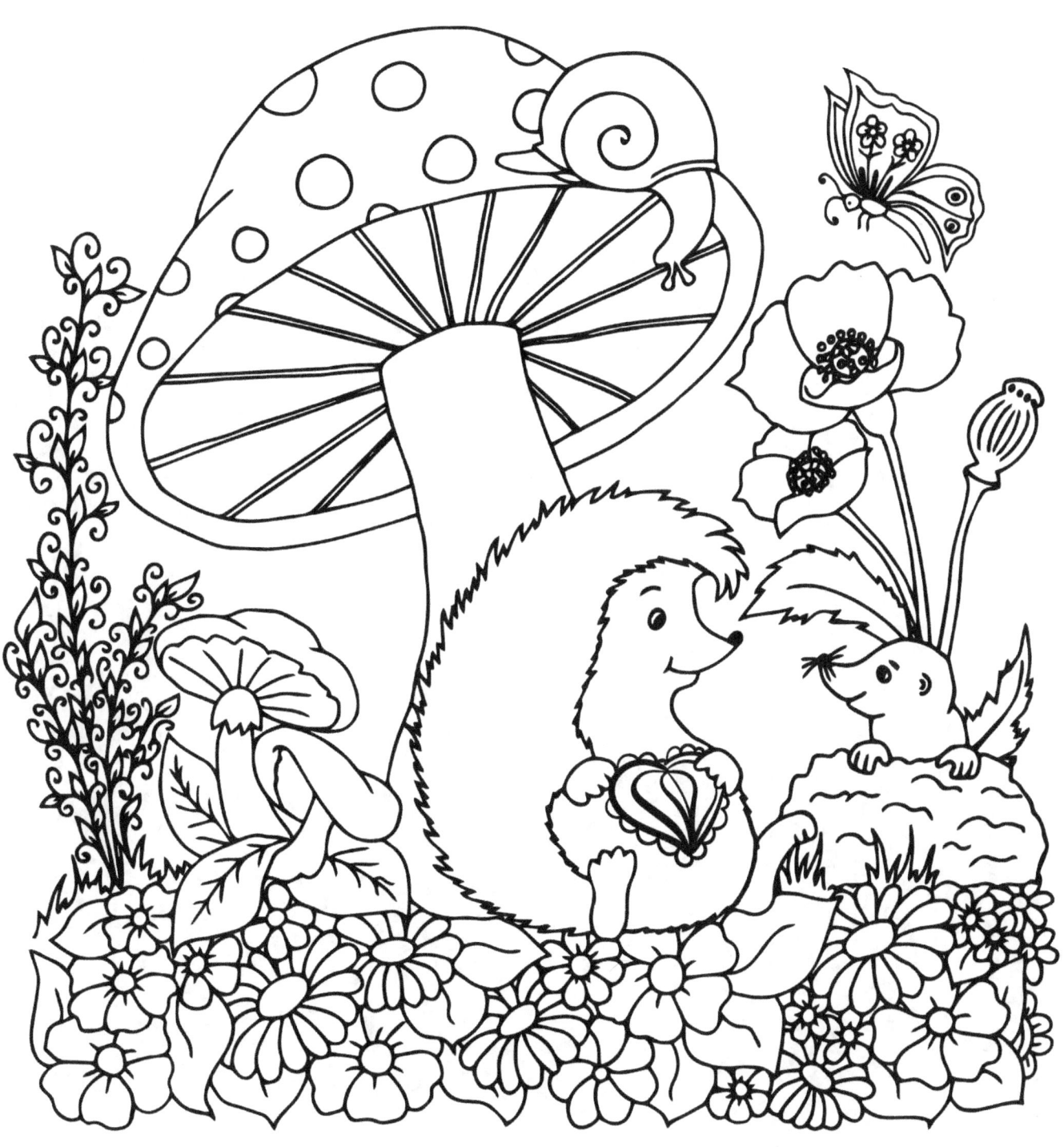

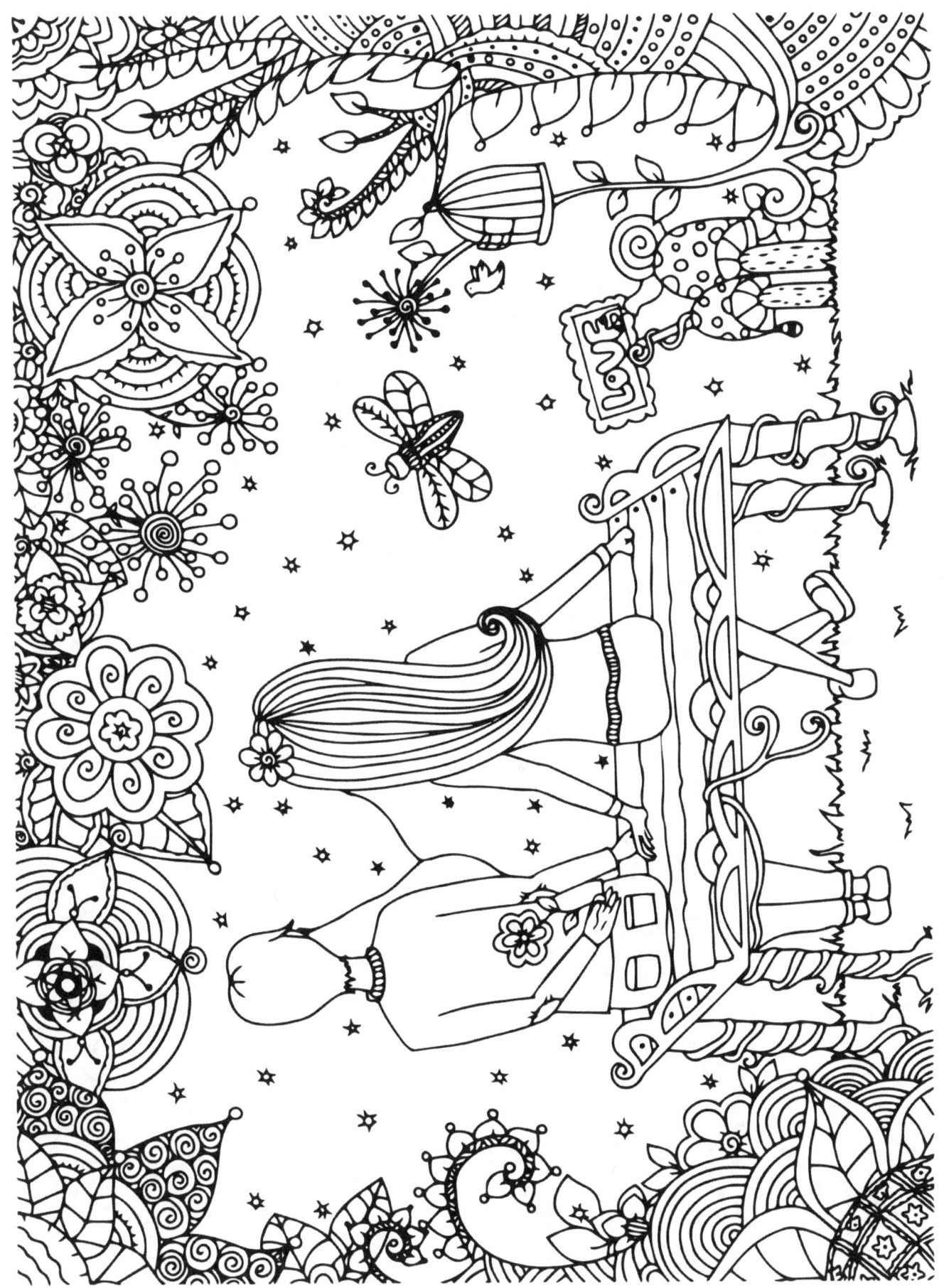

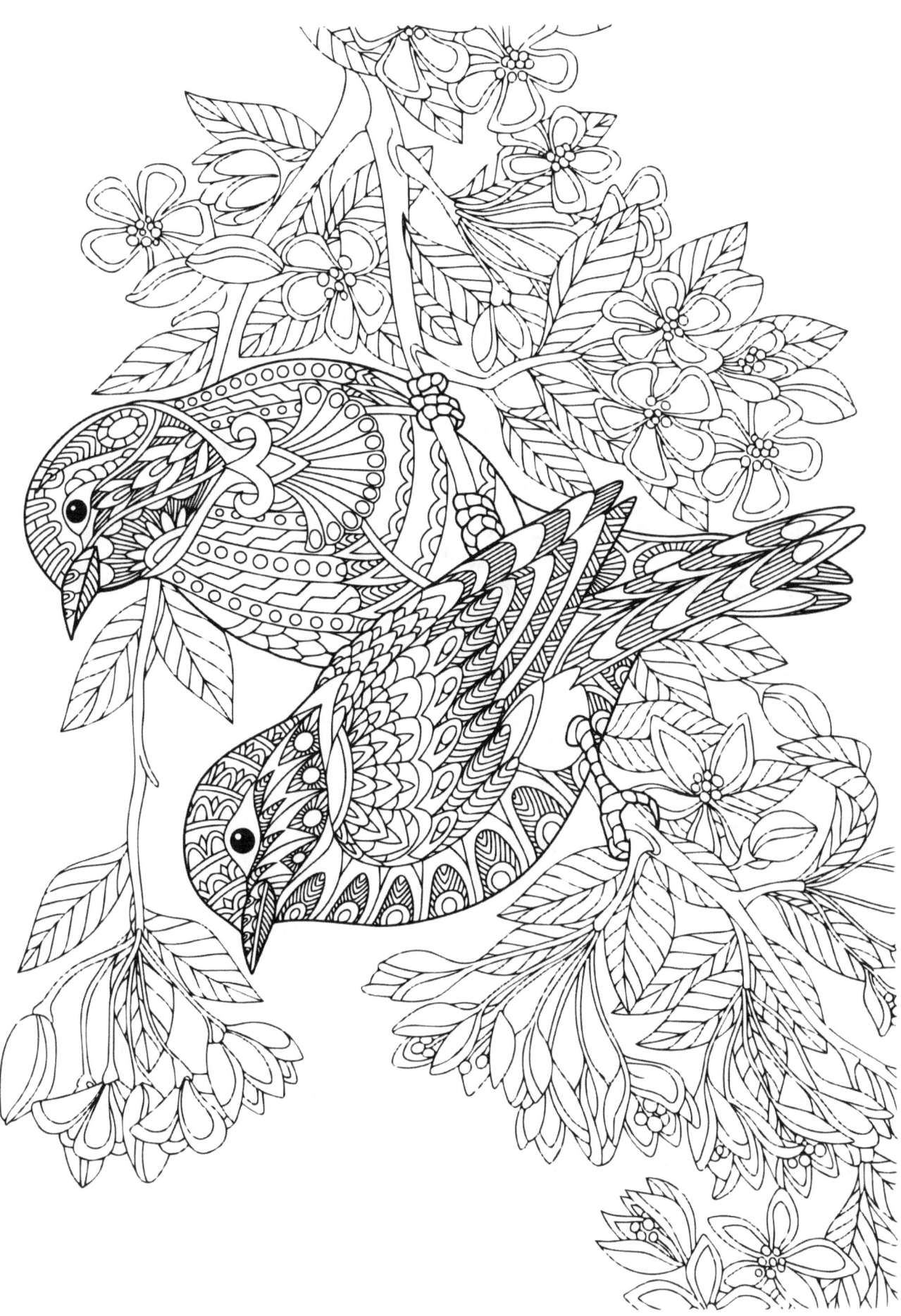

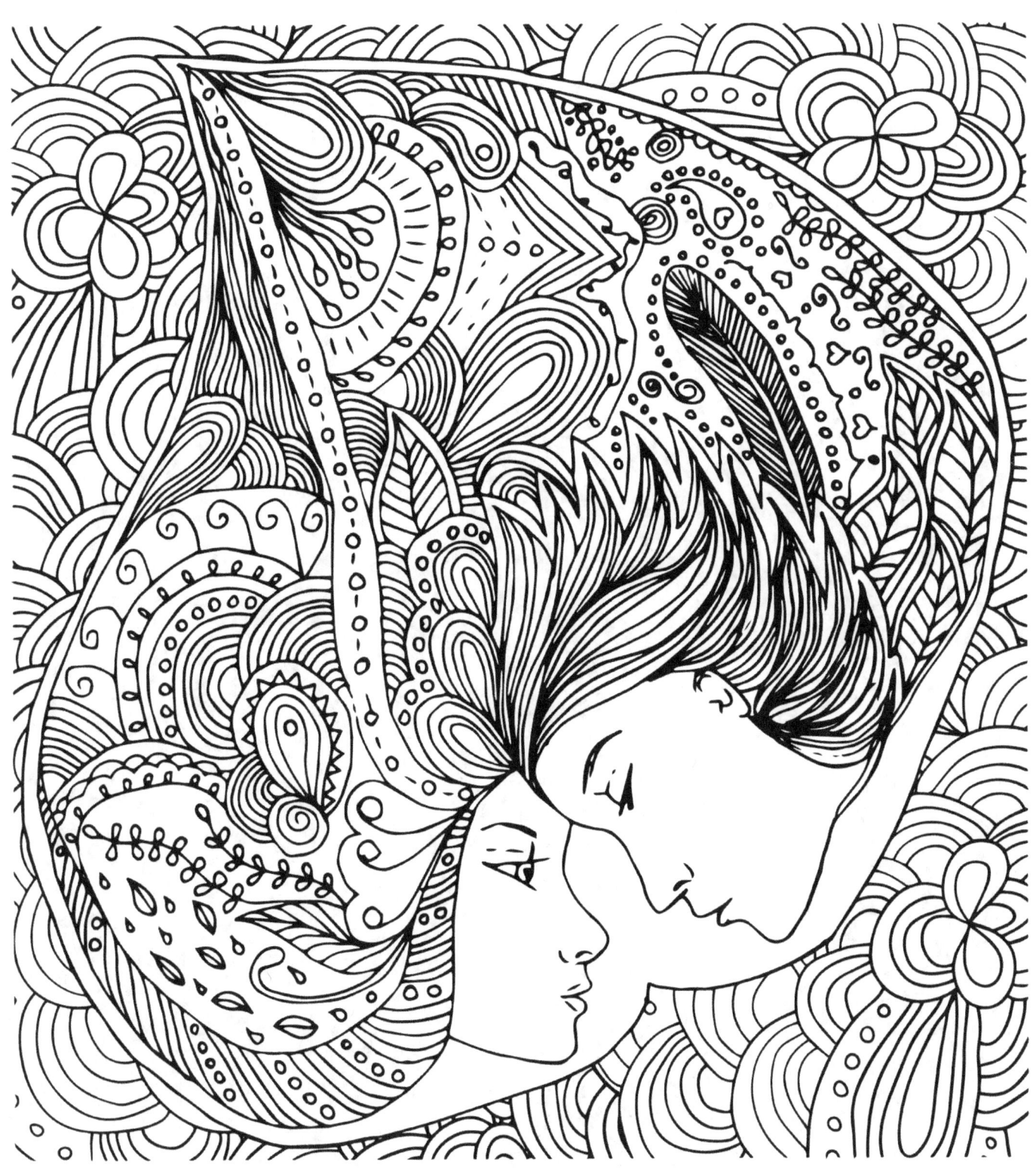

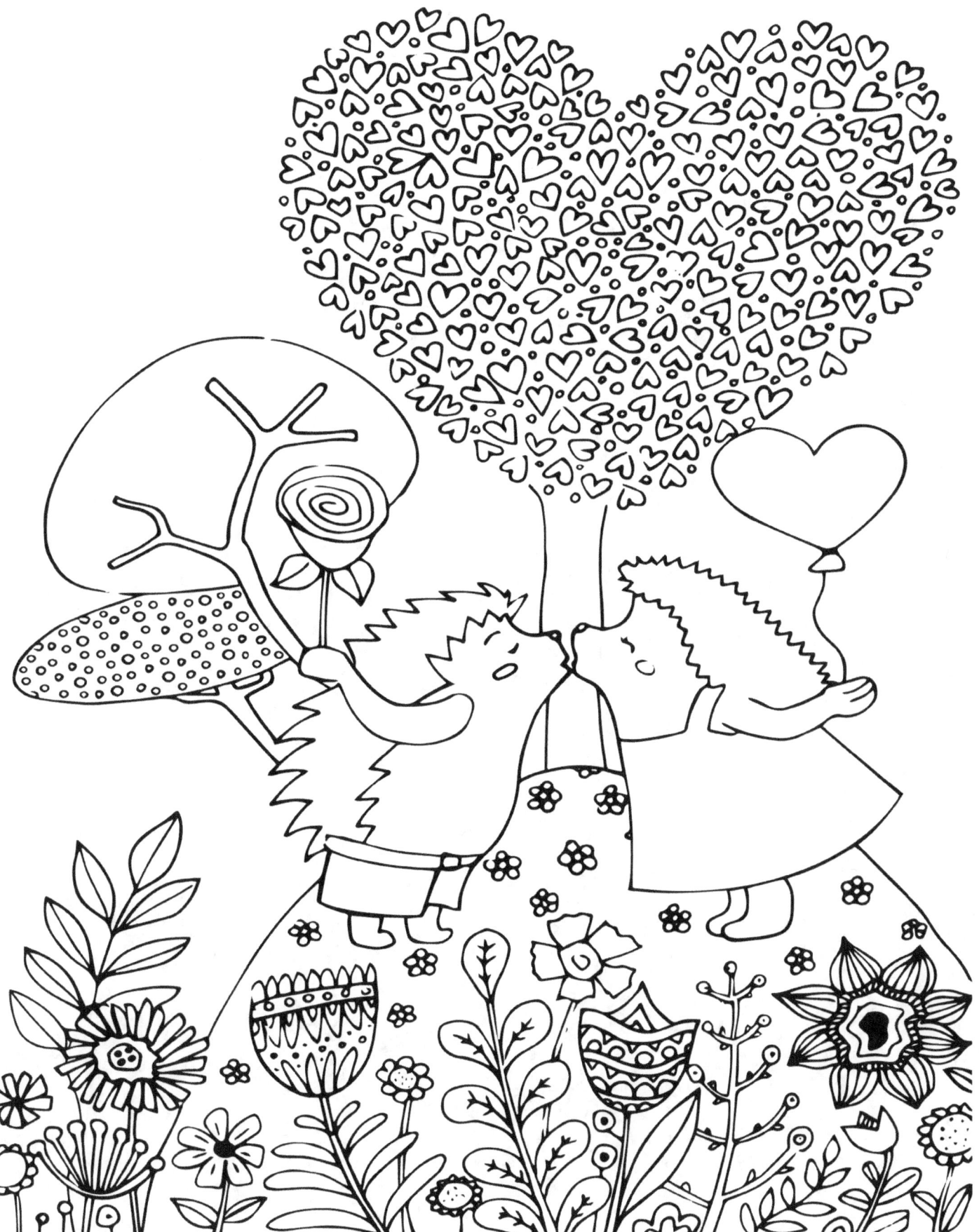

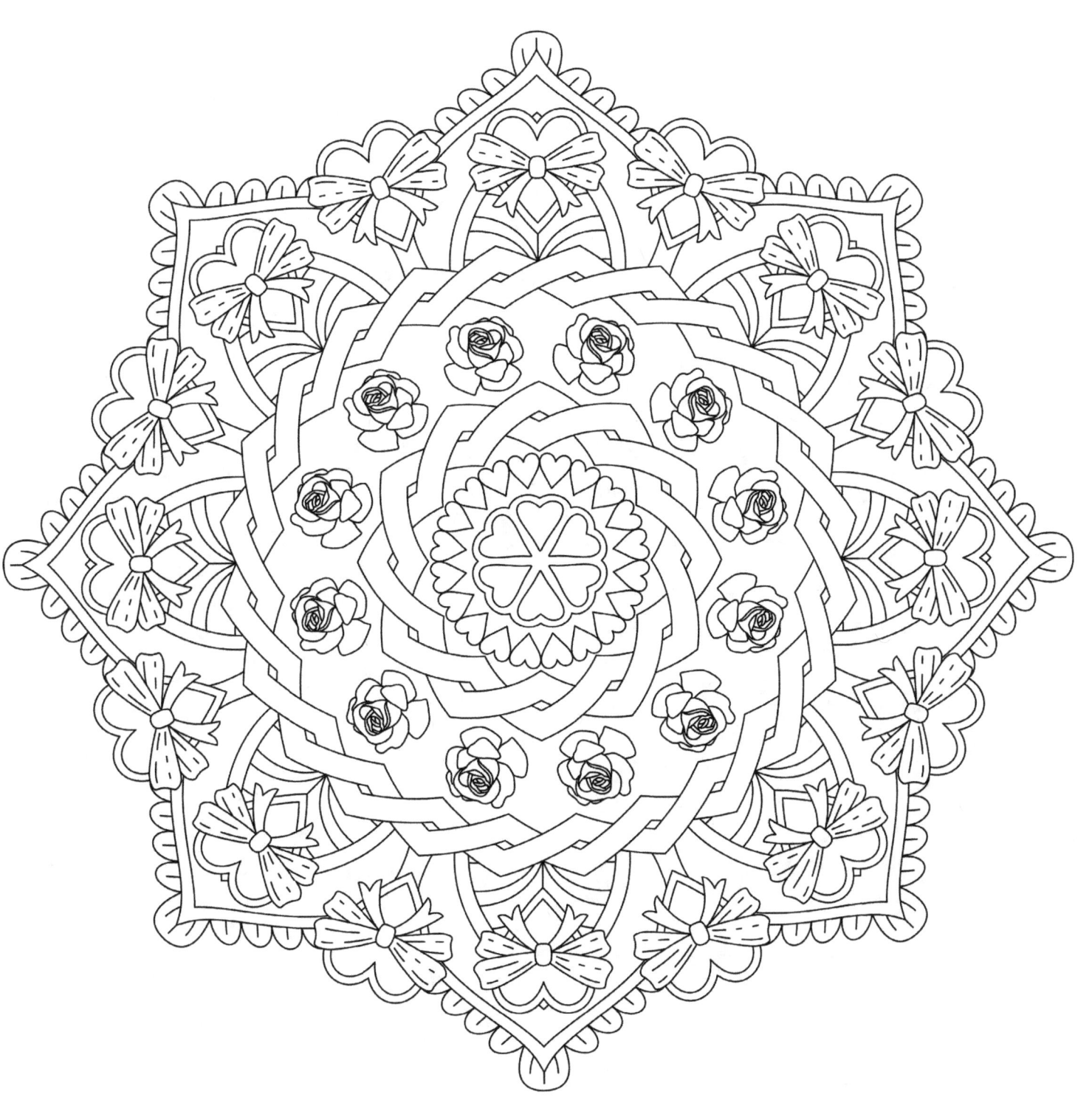

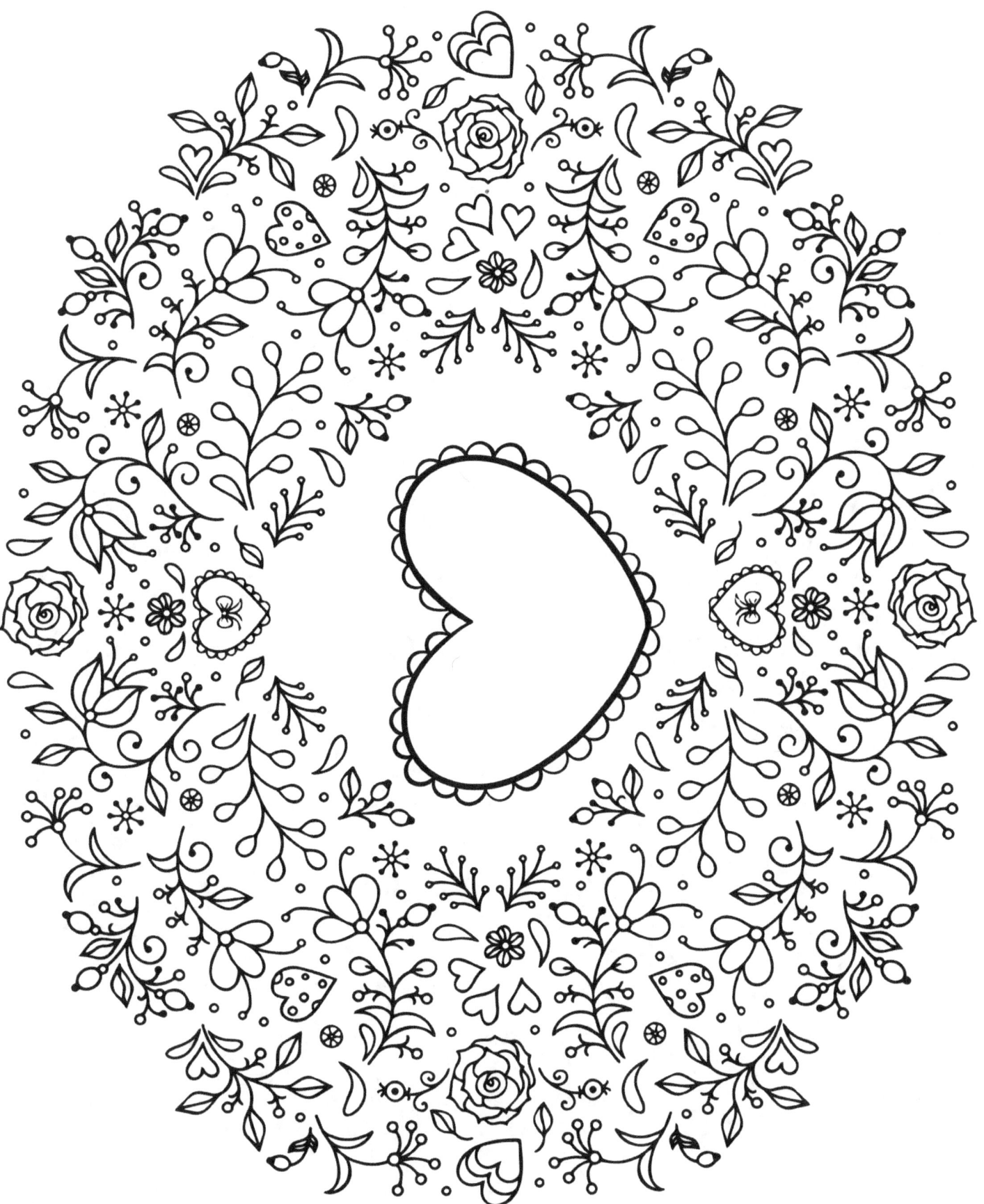

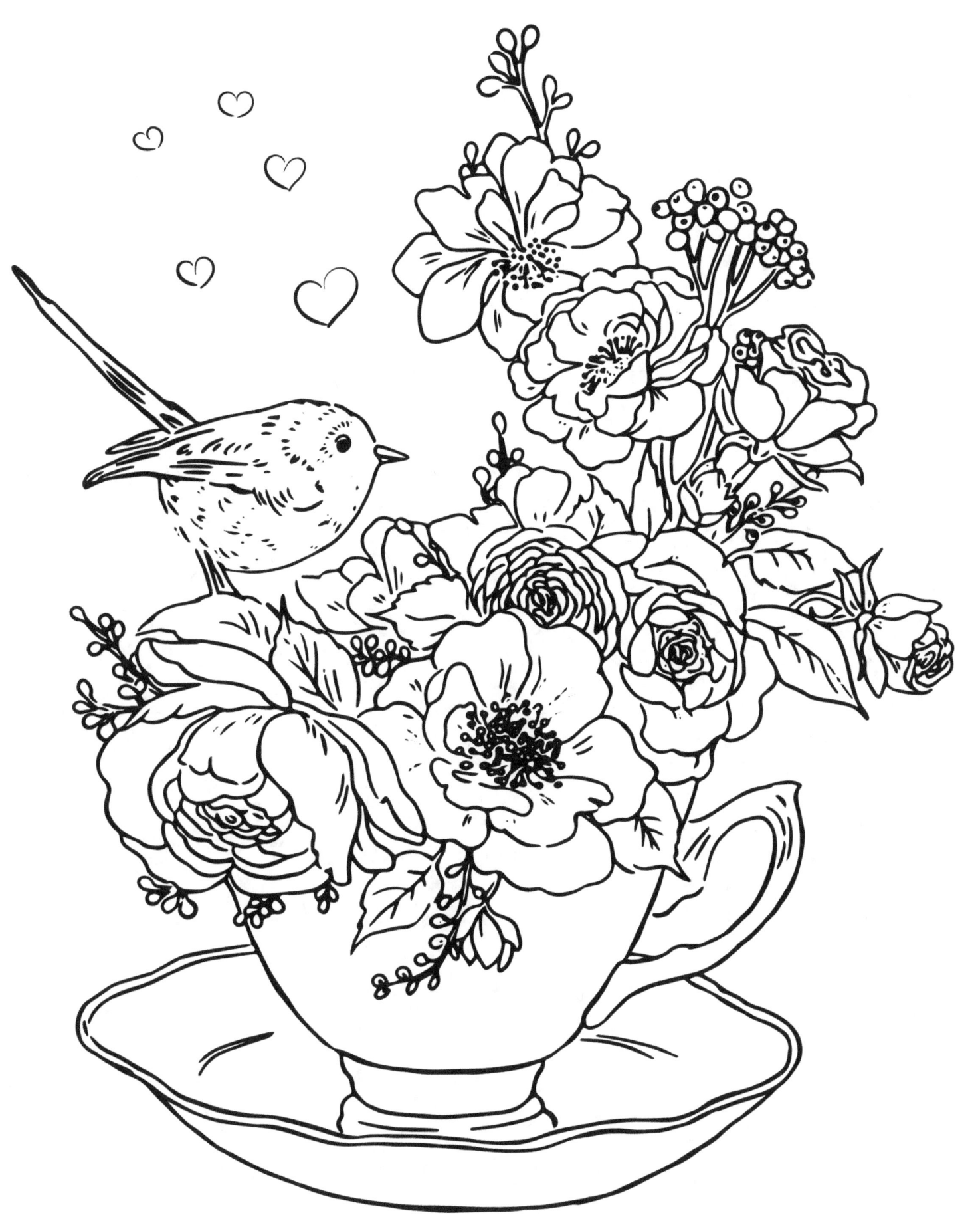

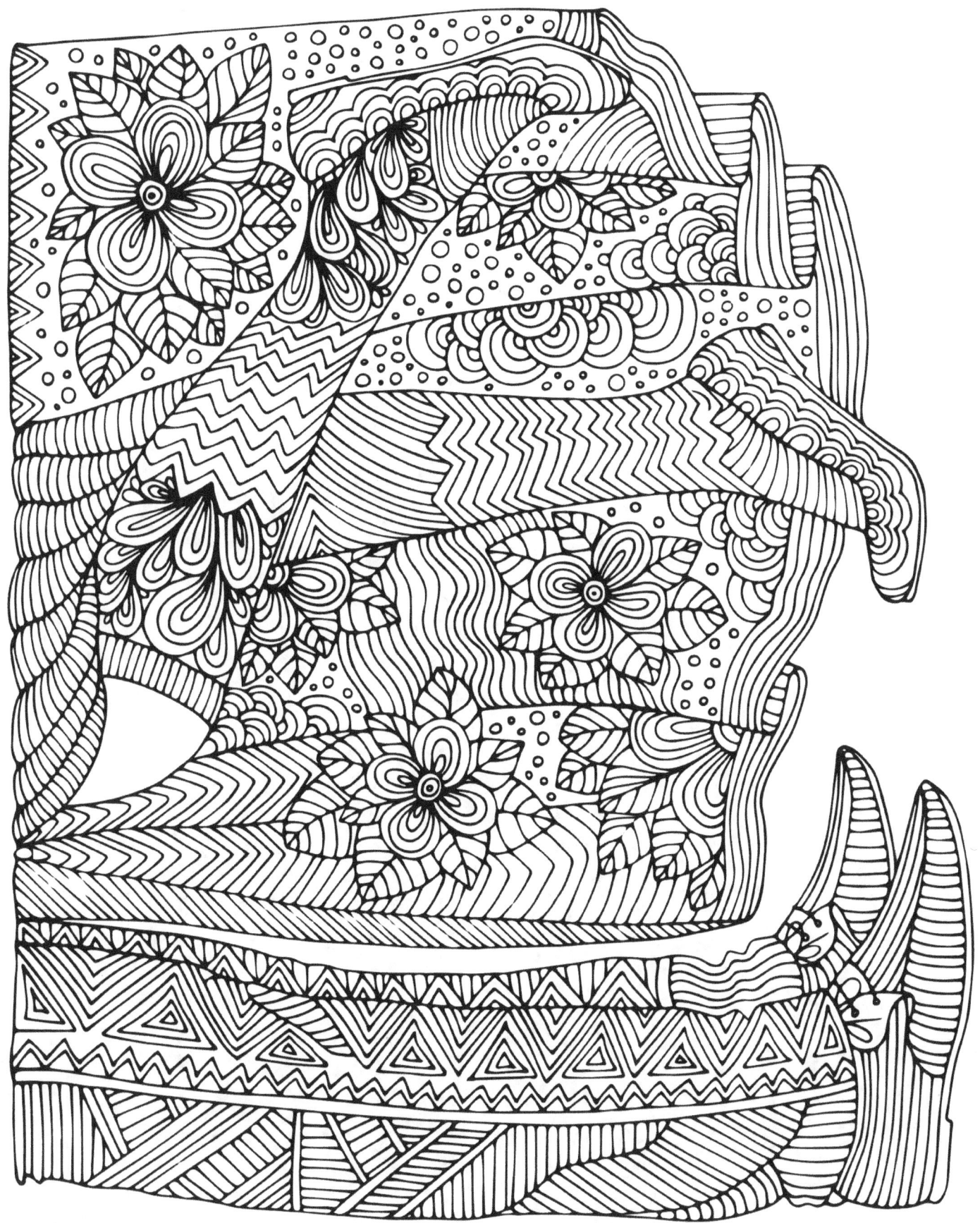

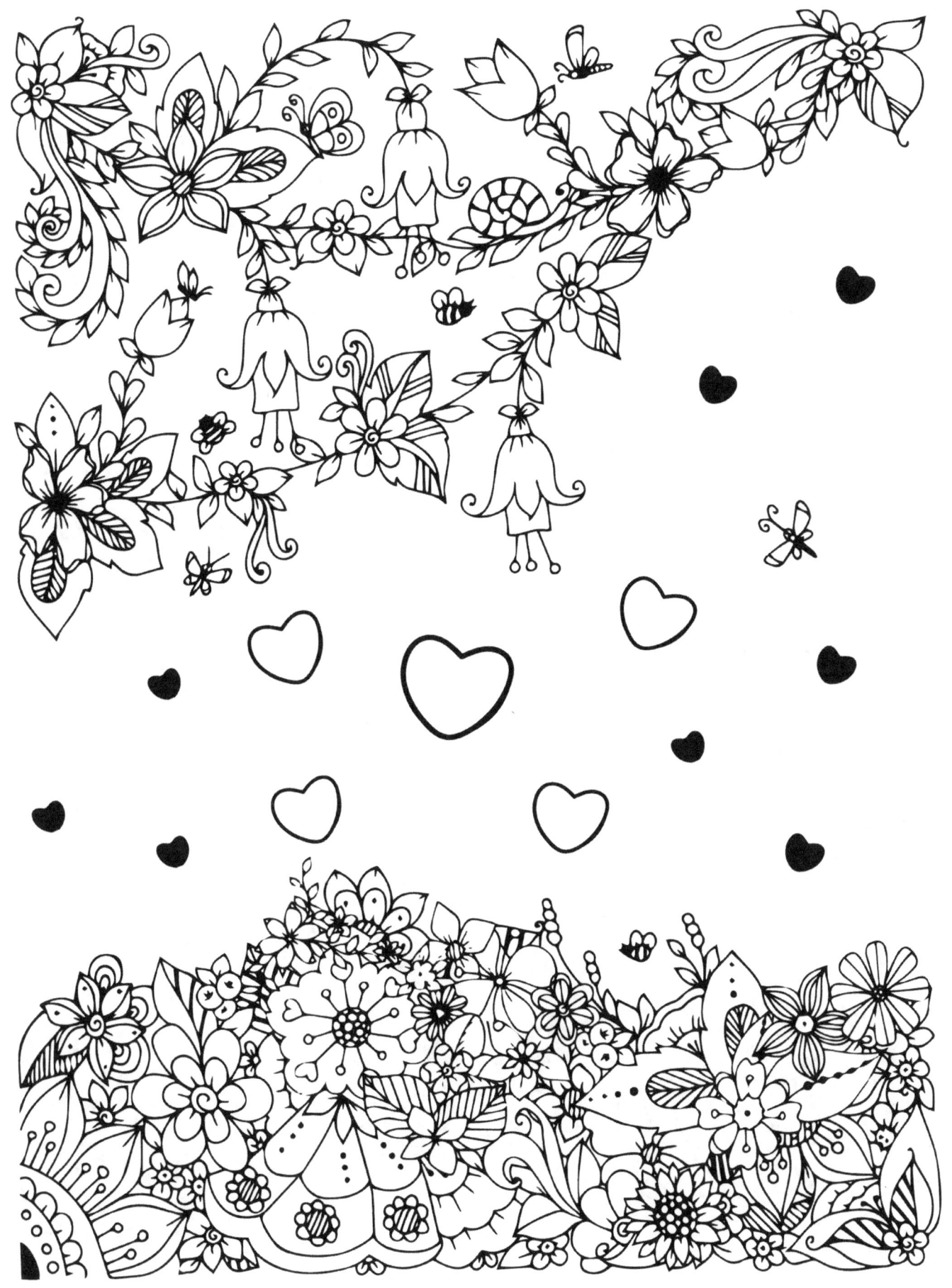

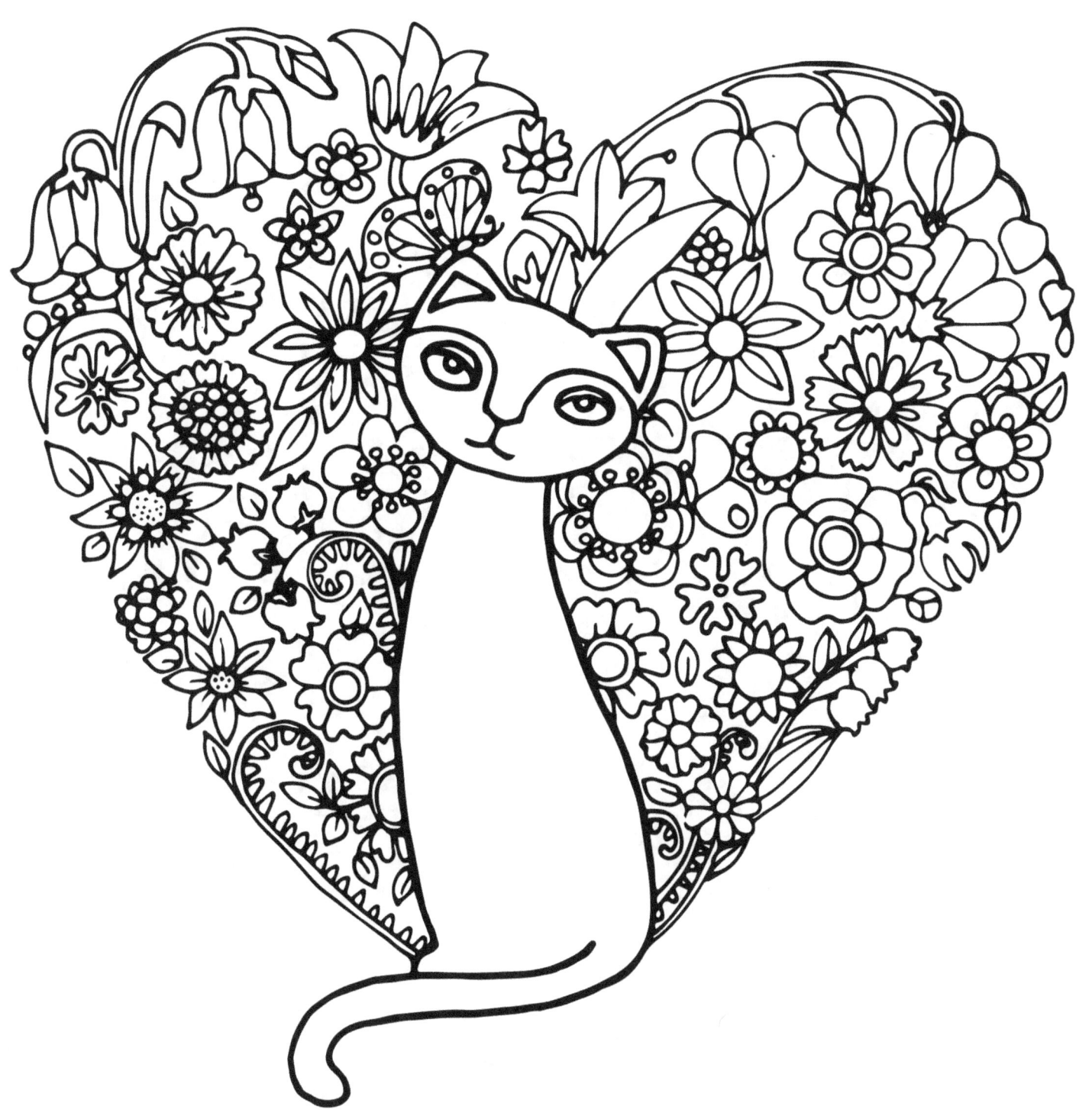

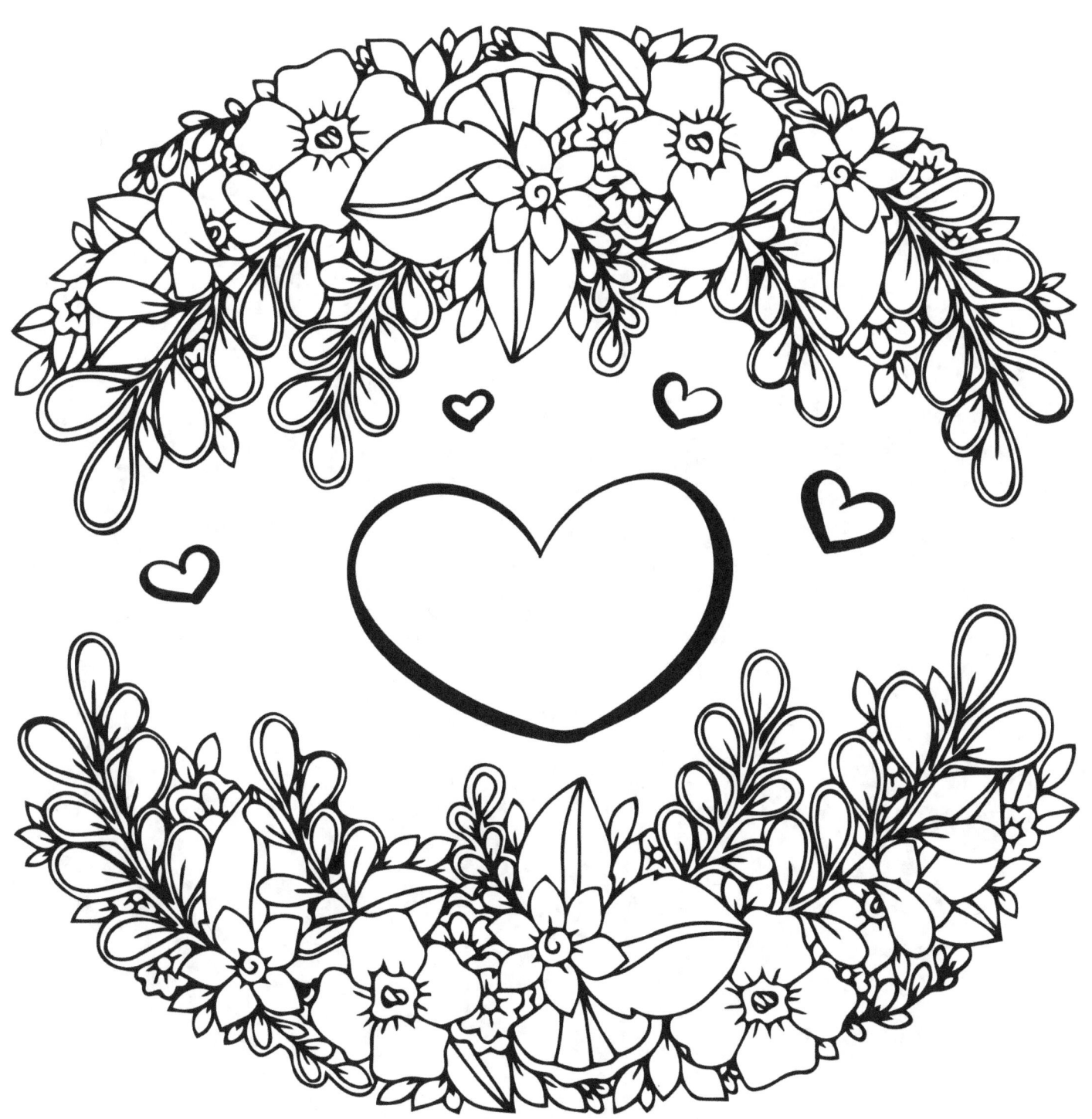

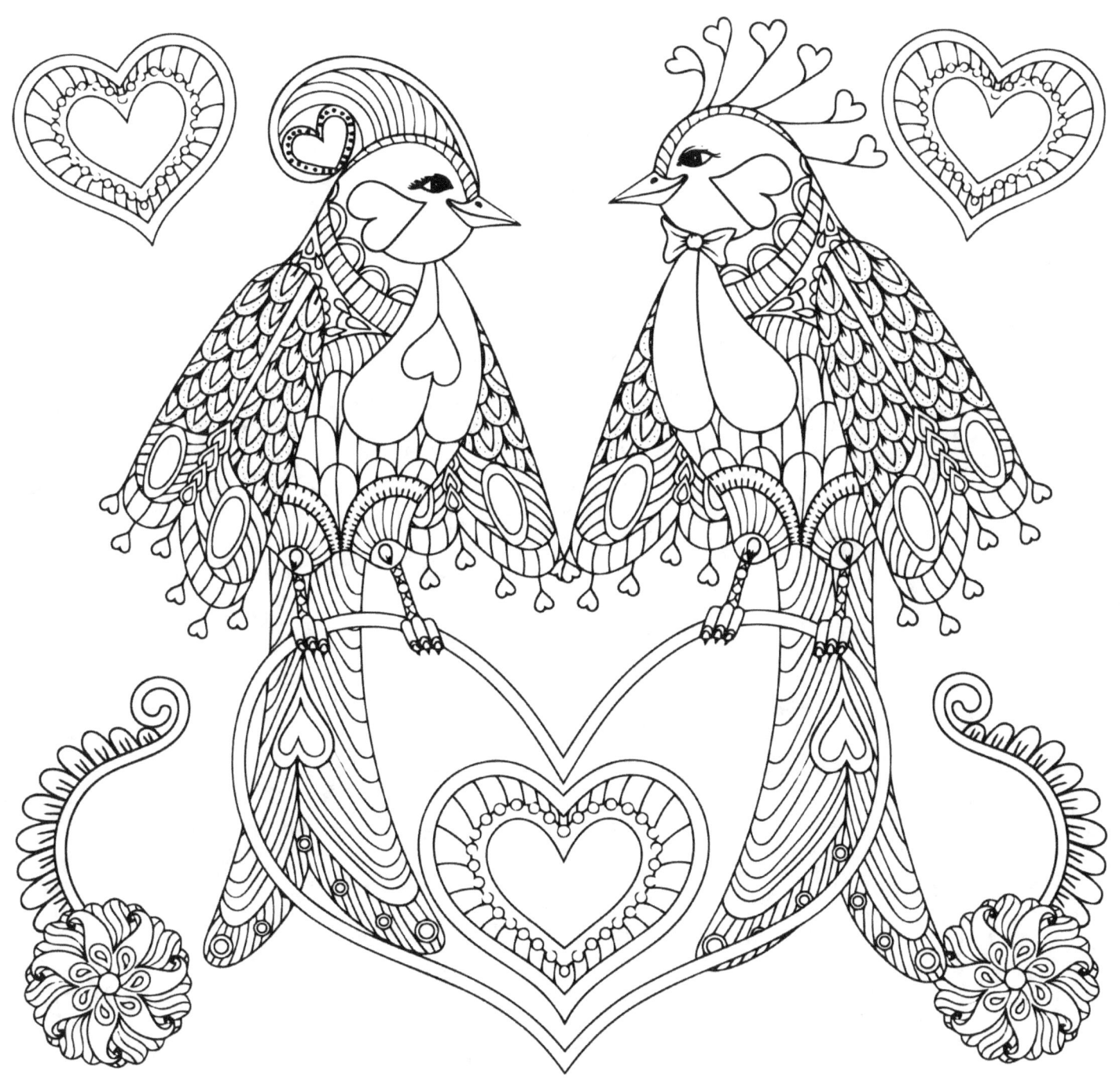

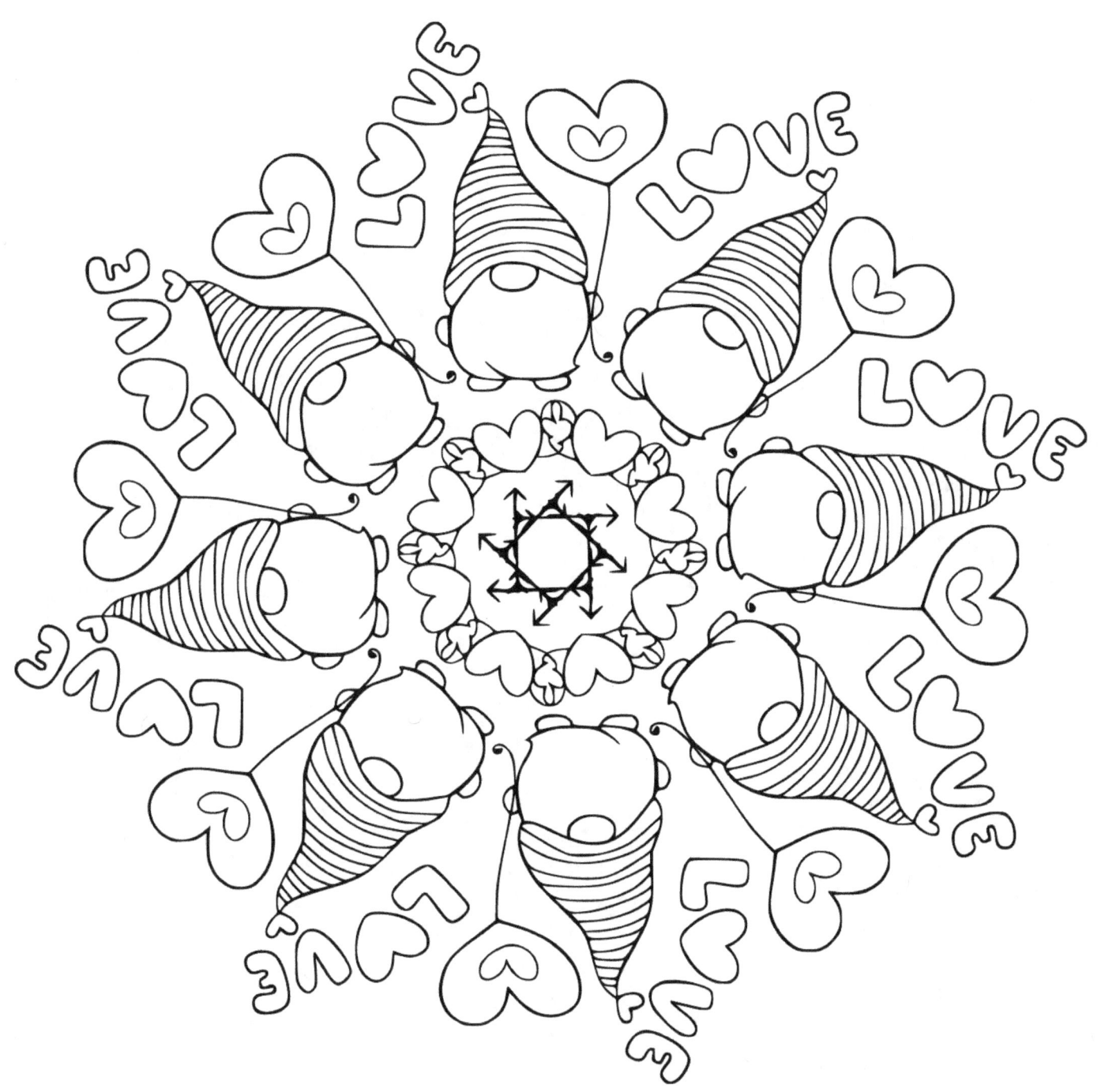

www.ingramcontent.com/pod-product-compliance
Lightning Source LLC
Chambersburg PA
CBHW081101240526
45465CB00026B/3020